Praise for *Is That Poop on My Arm?*

"The parenting life and the Christian life can sometimes feel like conflicting vocations: how on earth do we raise our children to love God and serve others, *and* follow in the way of Jesus, ourselves? What does it mean to live a faithful life in the glorious mess of parenting? Justin Lind-Ayres has traveled this road, and he is a wise and generous companion. He is also a preacher's preacher, the kind you want walking right beside you, all the way. This is a book of luminous writing, breathtaking insight, and (frequently) laugh-out-loud earthiness—a book to share and to treasure."

—Anna Carter Florence, Columbia Theological Seminary and author of *Rehearsing Scripture*

"As a new pastor and parent, I could not put this book down! Justin Lind-Ayres's *Is That Poop on My Arm?* will make you laugh and cry and give thanks to God over and over again for the children in your life. Lind-Ayres is a remarkable preacher and storyteller, inviting his readers to reflect on their own stories of heartache and joy. He helps us make sense of this wild world of parenting in faith—to celebrate the holiness of the messy parts, to listen to our children with wonder and curiosity, and to teach stewardship through the tooth fairy! I can't wait to buy this book for friends and share it with families where I serve."

—Anna Helgen, pastor at Mount Olivet Lutheran Church, Minneapolis

"Lind-Ayres dares to be honest about messiness, both the messiness of poop and the messiness of faith. Perhaps only parents will see the connection at first, but whether or not we ever have children, most of us know that the life of faith is often messy rather than predictable. The author is a gifted writer whose metaphors and descriptions open us to see ordinary experiences afresh.

Every chapter invites readers into these collisions between the mundane and the mysterious. Parenting while Christian isn't easy. Lind-Ayres, the parent/pastor, admits, 'It is easier to preach a sermon than it is to sit with small children during worship.' While the author has done both, he honors the challenging work of respecting children as part of the congregation, rather than sending them away so the sanctuary will be quiet. 'Maundy Thursday' startles us with the anguishing pain of loss and the outpouring of communal love. The final chapter offers one of the most poignant pictures of the communion of saints I have read anywhere. But you'll have to read to the end to see that picture with your own eyes."

—Barbara K. Lundblad, emerita, Union Theological Seminary, New York

"Lind-Ayres's honest storytelling illustrates a compelling portrait of a father embracing the vocation of parenthood and inviting you to do the same. He acknowledges the 'raw beauty, earthy grace, and love beyond comprehension' that characterize the best moments of parenting. He also has some moments where he definitely violates his household's rules about potty talk. You'll never view poop on your arm or spit-up on your shoulder in the same way after reading Lind-Ayres's unflinching account of parenting while Christian."

—Dawn Rundman, author of *Little Steps, Big Faith*

"*Is That Poop on My Arm?* is a touching and poignant narrative that successfully captures the beautiful mess that is parenting in faith. Justin Lind-Ayres seamlessly flows from parent to pastor, from prophet to student and always writes as an honest, vulnerable, and wise child of God. The chapters expertly and accessibly address themes from life and death to Cheerios and the Tooth Fairy, to stewardship and communion through the lens of precious childhood innocence. *Is That Poop on My Arm?* reminds us that our children are capable of preaching, teaching, and making our church better. They are, in fact, raising us. It is a gift to have faith like a child. I was pleasantly surprised to find myself both laughing and crying in the first chapter titled 'Poop,' and then I continued to laugh and cry reading every chapter thereafter. Lind-Ayres generously shares moments of deep intimacy with his children as they explore love, loss, giving, and belonging. He tells stories that are tender and true, oozing the good news of our gospel in ways both simple and profound. We get a front-row seat to moments between parent and child of blessing and being blessed, and in so doing, this book truly blesses us."
—**Ellie Roscher, author of** *Play Like a Girl* **and** *How Coffee Saved My Life*

"A decidedly honest, funny, and yes, messy book, *Is That Poop on My Arm?* is compulsively readable in every way. As a less-than-perfect Lutheran myself, there is so much to admire about Lind-Ayres's writing and candor; he's the kind of irreverent, thoughtful, and authentic theologian this world could use more of: unafraid to wade into the mess of this flawed world in search of beauty and grace. Thoroughly enjoyable."
—**Nickolas Butler, author of** *Shotgun Lovesongs* **and** *The Hearts of Men*

"Justin Lind-Ayres's *Is that Poop On My Arm?* is as funny as the title suggests and a great deal deeper and more powerful. The range of the book is vast, vacillating between the most mundane parenting topics, such as baby poop and the tooth fairy, and the most sublime faith topics, such as death, liturgy, and the Eucharist. Lind-Ayres weaves these together in a tapestry that is at once chaotic and seamlessly whole—much like real life. Ultimately, this story is a vulnerable, powerful testimony of one parent's journey of teaching the faith to and being taught the faith by his children. May we all have the wisdom to serve and humbly learn from the littlest, whom God has placed in our lives and care."

—Rachel Wrenn, pastor and PhD candidate at Emory University

"*Is That Poop on My Arm?* is a lively and thoughtful offering of true stories from the author's own experience as pastor, husband, and father. The insights that Justin Lind-Ayres offers readers and the real-life examples that illustrate them result in a beautiful braiding of the secular and the sacred that is by turns funny, poignant, and downright tear-inducing. Parents who are doing their best to raise their children in a Christian environment will find great encouragement and comfort in these pages. I only wish this book had been available when I was bringing up my kids."

—William Kent Krueger, *New York Times* bestselling author of *Ordinary Grace* and the Cork O'Connor mystery series

Is That Poop on My Arm?

Is That Poop on My Arm?

Parenting While Christian

JUSTIN LIND-AYRES

FORTRESS PRESS
MINNEAPOLIS

*For my children, Anya, Svea, and Soren, my guides
in parenting and in faith*

Contents

Introduction: Parenting in Christian Faith

faith (noun): 1. belief or a set of beliefs not based on proof (as defined by Dictionary.com); 2. "the assurance of things hoped for, the conviction of things not seen" (Hebrews 11:1); 3. the gift of God enabling us to trust in God and God's promises; 4. a lived journey of trust in the eternal love of God through the real tension of suffering and joy in life.

Parenting is a messy business—joyful, to be sure, but messy as hell. The same can be said of faith. A life lived in faith is rife with challenge, doubt, failure, anger, and heartache. Funny thing is, this description aptly characterizes a typical parenting day for me. When faith is combined with parenting, we double down on the mess. As a preacher in the Christian church and parent of three young children, I have learned that the sloppy intersection of parenting and faith is overflowing with raw beauty, earthy grace, and love beyond comprehension. The following pages offer snippets of my journey in parenting while Christian, my holy mess.

What you must know at the outset is that potty talk is prohibited in our household. Words like *pee-pee, fart*, and *poop* do have their place: the bathroom. Within their proper context, words describing bodily functions are allowed. But iterations of these words outside the confines of the bathroom are considered potty talk. As such, they are strictly out of bounds. So naturally, my kids like using them; they think potty talk is hilarious. Some of their favorite terms include *poopy face, poopy head, poopy nose*, and *poopy breath*. Add *poopy* to anything, and my kids will roll with laughter—that is, until the threat of a time-out is evoked. For my part, I find it slightly amusing when they use the term *poopy poop*. Describing poop as "poopy" seems redundant to me; I've never seen poop that wasn't poopy.

With potty talk off-limits in our house, I expect writing a book with "poop" in the title is somewhat hypocritical. No doubt, my day of reckoning will come, when I have to explain to my children my use of potty talk in this project. "Do what I say, not what I do" will not be enough. Someone may even call me a poopy head over the whole ordeal. It will be justified.

"Is that poop on my arm?" is not a question out of bounds when it comes to parenting, however. Spit-up on the shoulder, breastmilk soaking through a blouse, and unidentifiable sticky stuff on a pant leg are all markers of someone in the thick of parenthood with little ones. Turns out, poop is also in play for parents as a possible accessory to one's wardrobe. But more on that later.

Poop on the arm—or anywhere on the body—is both a literal and figurative way for me to speak about the messiness of parenthood in tandem with living a life of faith. Faith, like a baby cradled in one's arms, is a gift from God—exquisite, miraculous, fragile, precious. But a life lived in the fullness of this gift of faith is also full of shitty moments of heartbreak, self-doubt, and suffering. That is the rawness of living in faith that is both ugly and beautiful, crude and gracious, indifferent and bursting with love. We live in these tensions as a parent and, perhaps more so, as a parent seeking to parent in faith. At least, that is what I have discovered as a preacher-parent journeying with my parenting partner, Melanie, as we seek to raise three kids with faith in Jesus.

This book about the holy mess of parenting in faith will necessarily weave in stories of my three children: Anya (oldest), Svea (middle), and Soren (youngest). This is odd for me. Rarely—and

I do mean rarely—do I mention my children in my preaching. Sure, after a two-week parental leave and four-week absence from the pulpit after the birth of my first child, I mentioned Anya in my first sermon back. That was to be expected. What parent doesn't want to gush about the sublime perfection that is embodied in their newborn baby? Never mind the colic, sleepless nights, and constant feelings of parental inadequacy. Caffeine-induced compartmentalization is a godsend. Besides, I had a somewhat captive audience of nearly three hundred churchgoers; like it or not, they were going to hear about my sweet little daughter's intermittent snorting amid her uncontrollable crying fits. Just darling!

Nevertheless, these days, I seldom preach using illustrations of my three children. And I never share stories about my spouse; I'm no fool! Typically, my sermons go on and on about stories from the Bible. No surprise there. Yet I find myself sharing now, in this format, deeply personal stories of parenting in faith. Perhaps it is an excuse to purge the pent-up stories about my children and to safeguard them. When my memory fades, I will still have these words that trickled out from a cursor onto my computer screen from a reservoir of fresh remembrance about the joy and struggle of parenting in faith. But more so, I know for certain that this complicated journey of parenthood has strengthened my faith in God. That is, my kids have taught me more about the grace and love of Jesus than I could have possibly imagined. Even if I don't talk about them much in my preaching, my kids have enlivened my faith in ways I am still trying to fully comprehend. They are probably my best teachers in the faith.

So I humbly submit this compilation of stories as examples of the always-failing yet ever-fruitful task of parenting in faith. The pages herein contain stories that are earthy and tender, hard and painful, hilarious and entertaining. From the heaviness of death to the light touch of the tooth fairy, my journey (thus far) of parenting in faith aims to strengthen you in your own journey—in faith, or in parenting, or in *parenting in faith*. For I firmly believe that stories beget stories. When people open up and share stories from their lives, their listeners are often moved to become storytellers themselves. Stories then collide in conversation, offering opportunities for deep connection and intimate sharing. My stories are told to engender your own stories. As you read, I anticipate that stories will bubble up from within you, so that you may move from listener to storyteller.

Maybe you'll tell stories of your hardships in parenting and struggles in faith—"poop on the arm" moments. Perhaps your stories will be about your children, grandchildren, nieces, nephews, neighbors, or other people's children offering you a glimmer of the exquisite love of God. Or perhaps they are stories of your own childhood as you reflect on how God has been active in your life, creating faith in you. Whatever the case and from whence the stories, I hope in your reading you see anew how children in your life are sharing the wonder of God through their own faith, strengthening you in your own faith life. Our stories are the means to communicate faith—a lived journey of trust in the eternal love of God through the tension of suffering and joy in life.

In our storytelling, we take our cues from God. I believe that our God is a storytelling God. It is no coincidence that the biblical narrative is chock-full of stories. From Genesis's beginning to Revelation's final amen, this Bible is God's love story for the world, told in word and deed. Our recounting of God's story as we live in the tension of faith enables a similar collision of stories. I think of this collision as being like the confluence of two rivers—not surprising from a guy who loves fly-fishing.

Through the narrative of God's embodied love in Christ Jesus, the great river of God's story collides with the story of your life, forming an altogether new stretch of river. If you have ever seen a confluence of rivers in person or in a picture, you know that the colliding water often churns up silt and muck, creating a muddy mess. It's an appropriate image for the collision of God's story with our own, much like the mess of poop on the arm.

The word of God churns up our lives, revealing the truth of the hurt and brokenness in the world and within ourselves. Yet, despite the muck, the river flows on; we are swept along in God's story of mercy, grace, and new life. In fact, the turbid, muddy messes at the confluences of rivers are often teeming with life. So it is with us, so it is with faith, and so it is with parenting. Life, the real grit of life, is often experienced in the stirred-up messes of pain and heartache and brokenness. And that is where God meets us! This is why a God who meets us in the earthy flesh and blood of Jesus is, for me, the embodiment of true hope. For a God who knows your story—especially the shit-covered stories of suffering and muck of daily living—is a God who can redeem you.

It isn't all poop and pain. We find beauty and grace and love in this life of trust in God and God's promises. Parenthood has revealed to me the fullness of this messy tension of faith and life. I offer you my story of parenting in the Christian faith so that it may serve as a witness to "the assurance of things hoped for, the conviction of things not seen" (Hebrews 11:1). But a word of warning: keep alert as you read. You never know what might come flying at you!

1. Poop

eucharist (noun): an ancient Greek word meaning thanksgiving; 1. our response of gratitude to God's action in Christ as we gather at the table to receive the gifts of divine grace in bread and wine; 2. the time in the liturgy when, in thanksgiving, all are invited to feast on the goodness of God and are empowered to share in the redemptive mission of Christ for the world; 3. that strange and marvelous moment in worship when a tiny bite of bread and a thimble sip of wine fill us anew with the living Christ.

When our firstborn came into our life in January 2009, we naturally wanted to share the news with the world. A handful of photos of Anya were uploaded to Facebook within hours of her birth—a digital announcement for our day. We also opted for a traditional birth announcement via snail mail. But I was adamant about one thing: no numbers!

Neither the Facebook post nor the printed announcement of Anya's birth mentioned her length and weight. My one request to Melanie was that we *not* include these numbers typically associated with birth announcements. For whatever reason, it had always bothered me that we hold newborns like a newly caught fish, snap a photo, and brag about their measurements, as if to say, "Check out this lunker! I caught it trolling the birthing ward. Took a few hours to reel in, a real fighter. But look at the girth: six pounds, eight ounces, and a full twenty inches long. A keeper, for sure!" Perhaps the Minnesota fishing culture in which I was raised has tainted my view of this birth announcement ritual; nevertheless, I question the purpose behind broadcasting the numbers. So I insisted that we keep the numbers to ourselves like a secretive angler who refuses to disclose the details of such a glorious catch. Let us allow the photo to speak for itself.

Fishing metaphors aside, my distaste for disseminating the stats of newborns is rooted in our culture of competition. Though I understand that weight and length are critical measurements for health care professionals in their care of the infant (and the reason why my pediatrician spouse would care), the general public tends to treat these figures like the results from a judges' panel at an Olympic event: 6.8 is a decent score, but 7.5 is better. It feels to me that people compete with each other using the scores (falsely) as indicators of who endured "more" in her labor or whose kid is "healthier." Can we just wait five seconds before we subject our children to our world of constant comparison and contention?

In all likelihood, I am overthinking this. I am comfortable enough in my own skin to acknowledge my weird hang-ups. But that did not erase my very real annoyance at the time. Imagine my reaction, upon our announcement of Anya's birth, when all too many people immediately asked, "How much does she weigh?" For crying out loud! I put thought and energy into making her birth not about the numbers; regardless, the first words after "congratulations" asked me to treat my daughter like a freshly caught fish. To the questions, I wanted to say, "Who gives a shit? She is healthy and beautiful and precious." Instead, I said, "I don't know. Ask Melanie." And to this day, I still do not know the stats. (Melanie, of course, remembers.) In retrospect, it seemed that our intentional omitting of weight and length engendered even more interest among our family and friends.

In the birth announcements of our second and third children, we decided to stay the course and not include the oh-so-critical numbers. It might have been easier on ourselves to add them, because the questions continued. My response to these statistical inquiries continued to be blatant, prideful ignorance. This was my way of protesting against our culture's competitive nature. I suspect my tiny little protest went entirely unnoticed or was deemed another example of my forgetful nature whenever numbers are involved. But this birth-announcement experiment taught me that people, especially parents, pay attention to some things with exacting detail.

Take poop, for example. We all observe our own bowel movements to some degree. After all, they become indicators of general welfare and a healthy diet. It is good practice to pay attention to poop. But there is a major difference between observation and scrutiny, and as a parent, I have scrutinized my children's stool ad nauseam. Here's Exhibit A, a typical text-message exchange between my wife and me during our diaper days:

MELANIE: Hey, how's it going? Did Soren poop yet?

JUSTIN: Yes, he finally did. He pushed for a while. Poor guy.

MELANIE: Was it hard?

JUSTIN: Ya. It started hard. Kind of like rocks at first. But it ended soft and sticky. You can tell the Miralax kicked in. Had that smell to it.

MELANIE: Big or no?

JUSTIN: It was a good size. I've seen better. He seems happier now. ☺

MELANIE: Okay, cool. Thanks!

I would bet that if you scrolled through text messages between any two parents, you would find similar kinds of conversation—made all the more colorful with the advent of the poop emoji. As I envisioned entering parenthood, I knew dirty diapers would necessarily be involved. I had no clue how deep into shit—literally—parenthood takes you. It is safe to say that if you can describe to one another the color, size, smell, and shape of human feces through text messages, you are in pretty deep.

Beige with a hint of sunset-yellow, runny and wet, and a faint smell of stale popcorn: a classic breastfed-baby poop. These kinds of poops are sneaky and can be explosive. They may sound like a simple passage of gas, if there is any sound at all; however, many car seats can testify to the projectile nature of these poops, as their liquid form finds a way through diaper and clothes. I've often pondered the wild physics involved when a baby, calmly sitting in a car seat, barely flinches and sprays poop all the way up her back to the base of the neck, soaking the seat fabric in the process. What is worse, the lack of odor means you can drive several miles without knowing that the car seat has just been ravaged. These clandestine poops can strike at any time, including Sunday-morning worship.

I recall that happening when Soren was a few months old. He was starting to get some head control but still had to be supported at the neck. We were worshipping as a family at our home congregation, and Soren spent much of the service dozing in my cradled arms. Occasionally, he stirred. I attributed it to the guitar, drum, and piano that accompanied our congregational singing. The cause of his slight movements may have had more to do with his intestinal tract than the music. From my perspective, though, all seemed quiet as a contented baby snoozed.

The liturgy led us to the eucharistic celebration. Together we remembered that after Jesus had been anointed by Mary and betrayed by Judas, he took bread and wine—his very own body broken and blood outpoured—and declared, "This is for you. Do this in remembrance of me." We remembered, we gave thanks, and we heard the invitation to come to the table to feast on the promise. The people of God sang and celebrated the gift of Jesus.

Ushers directed us from our seats to the circle gathering

around the table. I gingerly stood up, not wanting to wake Soren. Following Melanie and the girls, we got in line to receive Communion. At that moment, I realized something did not feel right. Though Soren remained asleep, my forearm felt warm and wet. My first thought was urine. After all, I heard and smelled nothing. As our line moved forward to partake in the Eucharist, I oh-so-carefully shifted Soren to my other arm to examine the situation. "Wait. That's not urine. Is that—is that poop on my arm?"

My arm hairs were wet and sticky, there was a faint hue of beige, and to cap it off, there was a nearly inconspicuous whiff of popcorn. Yep, Soren had just shit all over my arm. My arm, his back, his bottom—it was everywhere. And having transferred his sleeping body into my other arm, I was beginning to register the dampness there, too. I looked at his face, content and innocent, wondering how one could sleep in that slimy mess. I wasn't prepared to wake him up just yet. As I had been told over the years, rule number one in parenting is never wake a sleeping child. There are exceptions to every rule, and this was a good one. But first, the invitation to the table of God was still before us.

With poop on my arm, I accompanied my family and the community of the faithful to receive the gift of Christ Jesus. The importance of this liturgical act was probably not at the forefront of my mind at that precise moment. Instead, my thoughts swirled around beige slime and how to contain Soren's sticky mess he had shared down my arm. For better or worse, I have paid an inordinate amount of attention to human excrement—a parenting hazard. Yet upon reflection of that parenting moment, I have come to realize a truth: we all come to Christ's banquet with some shit on us. At some times, it is more apparent than at others, but it is always there. We are all stained by life's trials and the imperfections of our sinful ways. My experience with Soren's intestinal explosion may be a metaphor for how we approach the table, yet it is still true. The power of God's invitation is equally true to us shit-stained people:

Come, my beloved children, come.

Just as you are, come.

Come, receive the mercy and goodness of your God.

Come, dine with me.

So, yes, poop and all, I heard the invitation and approached with Soren, my family, and the people of God. We all came to the heavenly banquet to dine with Jesus.

+ + +

As a person of faith and now as a parent, I have come to know the power of recognizing our imperfections. To put it more bluntly, I have discovered how essential it is for us to acknowledge that we will always and inevitably fall short. The church uses the language of "sin" to name the reality of the human condition and our inescapable propensity to offend one another by our words and actions. And though sin talk may be taboo in our culture, which strives for perfection on all fronts, there is truth and freedom in naming our shit-stained nature. In fact, if we begin with the assertion that we have and will fail one another, we can walk together in love upheld by reconciliation, restoration, and renewal. I found this to be true in my faith journey with God and God's call upon my life, and I have learned this power as a parent. This is where we ought to begin. When it comes to faith and parenting, there is no such thing as perfection. If we can begin here, then we can be honest with ourselves about the journey of parenting in faith as a journey not of perfection but of wholeness.

Since my parents brought me to worship religiously as a child and youth—and by "religiously," I really do mean "faithfully"—I memorized portions of the liturgy at a young age. While I was an elementary-school kid, I first learned the confession of sin. It would have been hard not to, really, for our family's congregation spoke the same words in unison nearly every Sunday. The communal confession of sin almost always happened at the outset of our worship, as we named aloud to God and to another our common truth. A good place to begin! And the confession itself almost always began, "Merciful God, we confess that we have sinned against you in thought, word, and deed, by what we have done and what we have left undone." To this day, these words or some semblance of them are often woven into the confessional rite. Their power persists. This confession is a catchall, the net of truth we fall into when our trapeze routine inevitably flops. No matter the airborne artistry with its flips and twists or our tight grip on the bar, the gravity of our brokenness will pull us down. There is no escape when all thoughts, words, and deeds are laid bare, and we are held accountable for even those things left undone. We cannot escape the fall; the shit of sin will mark us in one way or another. Indeed, there is *always* poop on our arms!

But when I get bogged down by churchy jargon and mental exercises of theological inquiry, I return to my children. They teach me what I really need to know about my thoughts and practices of a living faith in Christ. I really just need to look down to my arm. If I get stuck in my head, I need to visualize that massive diaper failure as warm, watery crap oozed onto me. I need to remember that moment and honestly ask myself, "Is that poop on my arm?" Upon closer look, the answer is obvious.

When I remember that sacredly messy moment as I approached Christ's table with Soren in my arms, I can almost feel the breastmilk-turned-excrement clinging to my arm hairs.

This is a memory that I need to cling to as surely as the shit had clung to me. For, humorous though the story may be in retrospect, it is a very real reminder of my failings as a dad, a spouse, a follower of Christ. Approaching the banquet of God while acknowledging that I am covered in the stink of sin teaches me who I am as person. That same confession of sin that I learned decades ago plainly states that we are "captive to sin and cannot free ourselves." This is my truth despite my want to deny it or weak attempts to cover it up.

For my part, I think about the times I have lost patience with my children and have made poor choices in parenting. This is where, as a pastor, I would exhort parents to have compassion for themselves. After all, I know firsthand that parenting is one of the most emotionally, physically, and mentally challenging tasks one can endure. And it is never-ceasing! But when patience has escaped me, I know that I have sinned against my children in thought, word, and deed. The worst of it, I think, is how I have taken my kids for granted and underappreciated the gift they are to me. That's probably my stickiest sin, if I dare be honest with myself. Too often, I get caught up in the mundane routines of parenting and fail to see the beautiful people God has entrusted into my care. It's a hard confession to come to grips with, as I see myself as an appreciative person. But the truth is the truth, and I am truth's captive.

I recall, painfully, losing my mind with my middle child on one particular evening. It was my night to fly solo and get the three children fed, bathed, and to bed. Engrossed in the routine, I failed Svea miserably. I was chronically sleep deprived, and my schedule became more important than Svea's wants and desires. Granted, they were not rational wants and desires, but she was three. Rationality is not a shining trait of a three-year-old.

With much of my attention on the needy one-year-old, I continued to ignore Svea's request to find one of her doll's small red-rubber shoes. While attempting to wrangle a nighttime diaper onto a slippery naked toddler, I told Svea that I didn't have time to look for the little shoe. It could be anywhere in the house, and we had already checked the obvious places. Svea could not let it go. She began sobbing, which quickly turned to full-on screaming. My head was pounding, official bedtime for the one-year-old had passed, and an epic tantrum had ensued. I lost it. I remember at my tipping point screeching at the top of my lungs and clapping three loud claps in a frenzied burst of fury, all in the presence of my daughter. If I watched this person on a video, I would not recognize him. But it really was me, frazzled and coming undone. Shocked and scared, Svea paused for a moment, looked at me as if I were a stranger, and began sobbing uncontrollably. So did I. Who had I become?

In these parenting moments, my sin is laid bare. There is a space in the parenting world where one should and, indeed, *must* have compassion for oneself. For me, this was not one of those spaces. I know better. Sleep deprived or not, I needed to be a fuller version of myself. Instead, my sinner-self had me captive, thereby squelching any saintliness yearning to be free. These are shitty moments in my parenting life, when I cannot see my children as sacred gift entrusted into my care.

The language and ritual action of confession in communal worship teaches us as a family how to seek forgiveness from one another in our daily living. When the pastor or priest publicly proclaims, on behalf of Jesus, the absolution of all our sin, we discover again the breathing space of the gospel. Jesus made this clear to his disciples by exhaling resurrection of life upon them. John's Gospel states it this way: "He breathed on them and said to them, 'Receive the Holy Spirit. If you forgive the sins of any, they are forgiven them'" (John 20:22b–23a). In this scene, the resurrected Jesus "conspires"—that is, breathes with—the

Holy Spirit, and the result is our task and charge to forgive. This is a holy conspiracy of the divine, forgiveness's breath. And in worship, we are taught how to breathe anew. We are taught to inhale the forgiveness of Jesus so we might exhale it onto others.

Upon reflection, I have found the rhythmic pattern of inhaling and exhaling to be a helpful way to see the organism of family life. But this reflection is made possible for me only through actual experience, an experience taught in worship and retaught at home. What I am trying to say is that it is one thing to reflect upon forgiveness and quite another to experience it. It is one thing to pontificate on grace; it is quite another to breathe grace into your lungs.

Sobbing together the night of my undoing, Svea and I shared a holy breath. We conspired together as our breath mingled with warm tears. I held her for a moment, watching her shocked expression dissolve in the familiarity of her parent's loving touch. Putting my hands to her cheeks, I looked into her eyes and said, "I'm sorry, Svea. I'm so, so sorry. Daddy should not have yelled. I'm so sorry. Do you forgive me?" And as part of our established pattern, well trodden in worship and in our home, this little three-year-old child muttered between staggered breaths, "I accept your apology." Her "accept" had a lisp and the word "apology" may have lost a syllable, but it rang clearly in my ear: absolution on the lips of a child. Nothing wipes away the shit smears more cleanly than such a declaration!

+ + +

To put it mildly, the church over the centuries has been a bit fussy about the theological understanding and practice of Holy Communion. Issues of contention include but are not limited to the following: What is actually happening at Communion? Who gets to receive it? How is Jesus present? What, if anything, do you have to believe in order to get it? At what age is it appropriate to eat and drink? How frequently is it offered in worship? Who gets to offer it? And how is it distributed to people? These are just a few sticky issues relating to this important ritual in the Christian faith. These theological and practical issues are reflected in the host of names given to this sacrament of the church. Do you call it "the Lord's Supper" or "the Sacrament of the Altar" or "the Meal" or "the Mass" or "Holy Communion" or "the Love Feast" or, my preference, "the Eucharist"? What you call it can emphasize what you believe about it.

For me, Eucharist names our unbidden and uncontrollable thanksgiving at the gift of grace freely and recklessly offered in the body and blood of Christ Jesus. Our thanks can only follow the gift. Said another way, without the gift, there is no thanksgiving. So, gift first. That is, the forgiveness, mercy, and love of God first come to us in the promise of Jesus Christ through the Holy Spirit's power. Our gratitude follows in the discernible path set forth by the gift. In the gospel narratives, Jesus gifted to us the bread and the wine with these words: "Take; this is my body given for you. Drink; this is my blood. Do this in remembrance of me." The command to feast on the gift of Jesus demands our remembrance. And in our remembering, we give God thanks.

Any parent will tell you it is a chore to teach a child to say thank you. You can drill it into their little brains thousands upon thousands of times. Upon receiving an act or gift necessitating thanks, we prompt our children, saying, "What do you say?" It is part of the training process to create polite manners, to be sure. But more than that, it is growing one's sense of gratitude. For the parent, it is an exhausting endeavor, for children tend to be sloth-like in learning to say thank you. Then it happens. As if by magic, a child on her own accord blurts out, "Thank you!" upon receiving a gift. It is a proud parenting moment to be savored. And it's short-lived usually, so soak it up when you can.

I think the eucharistic liturgy is God's training ground in gratitude, the regular communal practice of learning to respond to God's gift with thanks. You and I are really just big kids. Admit it. We too forget to give proper thanks in response to a gift. Now, compound that with the fact that what is given unto us in the Eucharist is God's own self in the body and blood of Jesus. How can one possibly comprehend this gift, let alone give proper thanks? I'm not sure we can; nonetheless, we gather to be trained together by the grace of God. Thousands upon thousands of times, the faithful gather to drill into our little brains our need to give God thanks. And at some point—just as it was for our children—our grateful thanks to and praise of God just happen. In community at the table of unmerited mercy and unconditional love, we receive God and express our gratitude as we learn to reflexively give thanks. Following Christ's command to remember the gift, we in turn learn to live lives of gratitude, sharing God's grace with the world. This is Eucharist!

It took a while for my eucharistic practice to reflect my theology in regard to a question posed at the outset of this section: At what age is it appropriate to eat and drink at Christ's table? Depending on who you ask, the answers will vary, even within the same congregation. For a long time in my denomination, a person had to be old enough "to understand" what was happening. Usually this meant age fourteen or thereabouts. I never agreed with this arbitrary age restriction on God's table. I myself received the Eucharist for the first time in the fifth grade at the age of ten—an improvement from fourteen, to be sure, but there was still room for growth.

While I was learning to be a pastor, many congregations began teaching "first Communion" at third grade. Again, it was an arbitrary age, but the trend was clear: guests at Christ's table were getting younger and younger. For that, I was grateful. But this begged the question in my mind: Was there an appropriate age when one ought to begin receiving? My heart was saying no while my head (along with the church classes) was enforcing yes. As a young pastor, I would teach classes with the title "First Communion" to second-graders (getting younger still). Though a year younger in my theological progression, the age still implied that there was a specific threshold associated with receiving the gifts of Christ's body and blood. In my heart, it still didn't seem right. I suppose I was trying to synthesize the church's practice with the words and actions of Jesus. It wasn't working too well. Jesus's words and actions were too persuasive for me.

In Mark 10, Jesus's disciples become annoyed that people are bringing children to see him. An indignant Jesus responds to his followers, "Let the little children come to me; do not stop them; for it is to such as these that the kingdom of God belongs. Truly I tell you, whoever does not receive the kingdom of God as a little child will never enter it" (10:14–15). Upon his rebuke of the disciples, Jesus then blesses the children, thereby allowing them to actively partake in the gift of God's presence. Though this scene is not specifically associated with table practices of the church, it does speak volumes to the import of children in God's eye. They are the inheritors of the kingdom of God and ought not be stopped as they approach Jesus. If the church confesses that the table of Holy Communion is the time when and the place where we ourselves meet Jesus, then I must take Jesus's welcome of children with utmost seriousness. He said, "Let the little children come to me." The church should echo his words in worship, especially as it applies to table manners.

If the tenth chapter of Mark's Gospel does not convince you, I hope the previous chapter will. There Jesus sat down, called the twelve, and said to them, "'Whoever wants to be first must be last of all and servant of all.' Then he took a little child and put it among them; and taking it in his arms, he said to them,

'Whoever welcomes one such child in my name welcomes me, and whoever welcomes me welcomes not me but the one who sent me'" (Mark 9:35–37). Without question, the children are welcomed and welcomed *first!* Between Mark 9 and Mark 10, Jesus's invitation is quite clear to me: children are expected, if not commanded, to come to Jesus; children are fully welcomed by Jesus; children need to be the first to come to Jesus; children are not to be stopped in their pursuit of Jesus; and if anyone is the recipient of heaven's gifts, it is the child in our midst.

These days, I find inspiration from the Eastern Orthodox Christian Church. They have been communing children—babies, in fact—as part of their theological understanding and practice of the Eucharist since the third or fourth century. That is, moments after an infant is baptized, the baby often receives a spoonful of the bread (in some edible form) and wine as a full participant in the celebration of the Divine Liturgy or Mass. As a pastor, I have yet to commune an infant; however, toddlers are regulars at the tables I have presided at in recent days. I look forward to my first infant Communion recipient, for "it is to such as these that the kingdom of God belongs."

At present, I support parents in their decision to enable their children to receive Communion whenever the parents believe it is time. It ought to be a family decision, not a threshold arbitrarily enforced by the community or church. My head journey about this Communion practice has finally caught up with my heart. As a church leader, I am more than happy to remove the "first" from the "first Communion" classes. Let's just call them "Communion classes," a time for any and all to come to learn, relearn, and discover anew the mystery and power of Christ's presence in the Eucharist. It would be a wonderful opportunity for intergenerational growth with Bible study and story, arts and crafts, and an examination of the church's Communion practices. Some class participants may be readying themselves to receive Communion for the first time, others for the 11,101st time. But together, the group would affirm Jesus's wide welcome and invitation to the table where all may taste and see the goodness of our God.

+ + +

Because this chapter has poop as a centering image for our theological inquiry into God's grace and our experience of Christ's radical and real presence in the Eucharist, it seems only natural for me to share a story about flatulence as well. These things are, after all, related biologically—and, I think, theologically as well. I'll let you decide, but the story is too good not to be passed on.

Following the worship service at our home congregation, I teach Anya's Sunday-school class of inquisitive and rambunctious elementary-school kids. It's a riot! The kids teach me about God while my co teacher and I try to keep their busy bodies occupied with a balance of Bible stories, art projects, multimedia materials, and genuine conversation.

On one particular Sunday morning, I was attempting to navigate the kids through a lesson on the disciple Thomas and his encounter with the resurrected Jesus, as described at the end of John's Gospel. This is the story that lands Thomas the unfortunate label of "the Doubter." For when the other ten disciples explain to Thomas that they have seen the risen Jesus, he responds, "Unless I see the mark of the nails in his hands, and put my finger in the mark of the nails and my hand in his side, I will not believe" (20:25). A week later, Easter Jesus appears to his disciples, and this time Thomas is present. Jesus then declares to Thomas, "Put your finger here and see my hands. Reach out your hand and put it in my side. Do not doubt but believe" (20:27). You would think, given his permanent epithet as "Doubting Thomas," that this disciple continues in his doubt. No! Thomas immediately believes. He declares, "My Lord and my

God!" This is one of the more powerful confessions in the gospel stories alongside those of the sisters Mary and Martha and faithful Mary Magdalene. If anything, Thomas should be called "Confessing Thomas," and I have preached a sermon or two with this exact point.

Now, I have nothing against doubt and its essential role in challenging and cultivating faith. I just have a problem with stigmatizing Thomas as a doubter when he is *both* doubter and confessor. We ought to affirm the importance of both and emphasize how they can happen within the same breath. That was what I was attempting to do with seven- and eight-year-old doubters and confessors—affirm both. So our little class was talking about Thomas, including the expectation that we need to ask questions about our faith in Jesus. In other words, questions and doubts are fully welcomed in the church. That morning, "Confessing Thomas" became our pathway to theological inquiry of faith and doubt, second-grade style.

Midway through the class, sweet Linnea posed a question about Jesus I had not anticipated. I had lost control of the class a bit as questions about Jesus had spun off to several side conversations. As a couple of the boys debated the wounds of Jesus's hands and side and the potential for gore, Linnea muttered a quiet question to herself and began to giggle. Her grin remained fixed on her seven-year-old face as she pondered her own theological query. I ignored the boys and blood talk for the moment and had to ask, "Linnea, did you have a question?" She did.

Without making eye contact and looking straight ahead as if still engaged in a self-entertaining conversation, Linnea stated, just loud enough so only I could hear her, "I wonder what Jesus's farts smelled like." At that moment, I fully understood her giggles and the wide grin upon her face. Jesus's farts? Hmm, I'm quite certain my theological training never covered the topic of Jesus's gas. And it certainly wasn't in our Sunday-school curriculum materials for the day. In the past, I had slipped into a Christmas sermon the real and immediate need for Mary and Joseph to deal with baby Jesus's poopy britches. That detail delivers a vivid incarnational message, I think, as we seek to grasp the weight of God taking on the fullness of humanity. But the farts of an adult, thirty-year-old Jesus? The Son of God—Light from Light, True God from True God—breaking wind? It hadn't occurred to me until Linnea wondered it aloud.

I'll just be honest: I am proud of my response to her. I could have made the mistake of laughing at her question—and trust me, I was laughing on the inside. But laughing at the legitimate questions of children, even the intentionally silly ones, can send the wrong signal to budding learners. After I shook off my surprise and securely hid my own grin, I embraced the incarnational nature of Linnea's question and said, "I suppose Jesus's farts smelled a lot like yours, Linnea." Theologically speaking, I was trying to connect Linnea to Jesus in an earthy way that fully revealed the humanity of our God. Practically speaking, I was trying to emphasize that farts are no big deal, as we all pass gas.

Linnea continued to look straight ahead, perhaps embarrassed that we were talking about farts. More likely, she was caught up in the humor of it all. Her response to my retort was perfect. For when I said, "I suppose Jesus's farts smelled a lot like yours, Linnea," Linnea replied, "My farts are stinky."

Now, at that part, I had to work overtime to suppress my laughter; much like suppressing a fart at the wine-and-cheese party with friends, it was nearly impossible. But I wasn't going to cave in, and the laugh remained bottled up inside. Linnea's face, however, continued to hold her sheepish grin as she named the truth of her bodily function while giggling. Thank you, "Confessing/Doubting Thomas," for allowing us to ask questions of faith, even questions regarding Jesus's flatulence. Affirming Linnea's question, I responded to her truth-sharing moment with my own certitude. I said to her, "Jesus's farts were stinky, too, Linnea. Just like yours and mine."

+ + +

With poop on my arm, confession on my lips, and perhaps farts in the air, I acknowledge that the invitation of Jesus to come and dine with all his beloved children is more genuine than I will ever fully realize during my pilgrimage on earth. I get it, but not completely. The moment we eliminate space for the mystery and wonder of God offered in the simple bread and wine of our eucharistic meal is the moment we cease recognizing the real and radical presence of Jesus. When Jesus said of this bread and wine, "This is my body; this is my blood given for you," we were invited to taste the mystery of grace, no matter our faults of thought, word, and deed. The result? Thanksgiving and celebration in the goodness of our God!

One Sunday some time ago, our family joined God's people of our worshipping congregation at the table of Jesus, per the weekly norm. Our girls, probably six and four at the time, had a serious case of the sillies. In public worship, I prefer a case of the sillies to a case of the stinkers. Typically, I'd rather see my kids giggling together than wrangling with one another; still, a persistent case of the sillies can wear on a parent's nerves after a while, because it usually means that any semblance of listening has given way to laughter. I remember feeling my annoyance level rising as the girls' sillies accompanied them to Christ's table.

By this point, both girls had been receiving Communion for some time. Anya began at the age of three, while Svea received at two. As is often the case in family life, the younger child gets to do things at an earlier age than the older. Firstborn children everywhere decry the "injustice" of it all, even as they spitefully play the "no fair" card, with tears and the slamming of doors being optional, albeit effective, points of emphasis. The loosing of age restrictions really isn't an intentional affront by the parents to the sensitivities of the older child. I just think parents tend to overthink everything with the firstborn; therefore, by the time another kid or two comes along, there has been a serious encroachment of space for such sustained mental energy—not to mention the physical energy as well. As a second-born child myself, I am grateful my older brother paved the way for me, so that I could eat sweets, stay up later, and watch PG movies all at an earlier age than he was. Shane: you have my smug yet genuine thanks! Someday Svea may thank her sister for the privileges Anya essentially earned her, but I doubt it.

Allowing Svea to partake in the Eucharist earlier than her sister was a no-decision decision on our part, I think. It seemed like we couldn't find any reason to make her wait for some arbitrary age because we had done so with Anya. On this particular Sunday, then, both girls were steeped in the rhythm of the ritual practice. They knew to pick up the small pottery cups prefilled with grape juice and take our turn in the circle around the table in the center of our worship. We joined some thirty other doubters/confessors of Jesus in the circle. The divine mystery was unfolding all around us, and the girls were embracing their case of the sillies.

After the girls received the bread, Pastor Erik stooped to their level, looked at their prefilled cups and then into their eyes, and declared to each of them, "The blood of Christ shed for you." The smirks were evident on their faces as the sillies slipped out the sides of their mouths. When Pastor Erik walked on to the family communing next to us, Anya turned to Svea with a mischievous twinkle in her eye. Anya lifted her pottery cup to her sister as if she were in a pub and said quite loudly, "Cheers!" Svea giggled, clanged her cup against her sister's, and repeated back a glad "Cheers!" They then shared a quick giggle before simultaneously slamming their shots of grape juice as if they were on the second leg of a bar crawl. My instinctive parental emotive response was embarrassment fused with frustration, for my (false) perception of proper decorum at the Communion table had been shattered by these two silly girls. I felt a swift response coming from within the chambers of my parenting self.

But then I took a breath—a small, simple breath.

It was just enough to put in check my knee-jerk parental habits and actually think about this situation. I looked at these girls grinning with unabashed joy and realized I was the one being absurd. My frustration and annoyance sloughed away. Here were two girls partaking in the Eucharist with exuberant merriment, as if at a party. And were we not a party? Was this not a joyous table gathering where Jesus as host serves a heavenly banquet rich with mercy and dripping with grace? Was this not a celebration of divine gifts beyond human comprehension? Maybe my girls were onto something with their clinking cups. Perhaps our response to the bread and wine should not always be held back by ritualized protocol and procedures. Rather, what if the Holy Spirit sends us the sillies as we celebrate the sacrament of God's very presence among us?

I remember looking up from my daughters at the circle of folks celebrating with us. I know for certain that one woman heard and saw everything. She had a delicious smile on her face; her eyes were aglow with amusement. Apparently, the girls' joy was contagious. At that moment, I should have lifted my own glass in the woman's direction across the circle from me and mouthed a "cheers" at her. Instead, I smirked as the sillies began to infiltrate my body. Anya and Svea got it. It took me a moment, but I think I got it, too.

It was in that same circle formation that Soren got it, though his time came a little while thereafter. Soren was sixteen months old. I remember because he still wasn't walking and was a lug to carry around. I attribute it in part to third-child laziness; after all, he had four people willing to do his beckoning. Who needs to walk when you can get what you want with a point and a yell? (All our kids were late walkers, though, so who knows why it took him so long to walk.) But on this particular Sunday, I held Soren—poop-less this time!—as we gathered in the familiar Communion circle.

Soren watched from my arms as everyone in the circle was receiving the bread-body of Jesus. He was used to the scene, since he had been doing it from the beginning of his days, when pooping on Dad's arm was a thing. But on this day, something clicked for Soren. I attribute it to the wide welcome of Christ's table expressed by our home congregation and their intentional insistence on children's participation in the breadth and depth of worship. As Pastor Stephanie approached us with the bread, Soren put out his hand. He wanted it. Pastor Stephanie looked at Soren and then at me. I gave her a half shrug and unconvincingly whispered, "He doesn't receive yet." Confident in her sacramental theology and reading the situation, Stephanie in her pastoral wisdom and parenting sensitivities looked at Soren's outstretched hand and declared, "He does now! This is the body of Christ given for you, Soren." Soren looked at the chunk of soft bread in his hand—the very gift of God for him—and promptly gobbled it up, arbitrary age be damned! Soren got it. Thanks to Pastor Stephanie's rootedness in the radical grace of God, Melanie and I didn't have fuss over when to "allow" Soren to receive Communion. Soren got it, Stephanie knew it, and it was given to him in faith, trusting in Christ who proclaims, "Let the little children come to me."

I am starting to get it more and more each day.

2. Snack

liturgy (noun): from the Greek *leitourgia*, meaning "the work of the people," that is, a public work for the sake of others; 1. the rites, rituals, and ceremonials of corporate worship; 2. the rhythm of the Christian faith—the fleshy enactment of the grace of God—that enables people to live out the mission of Christ Jesus for the sake of the world.

I became a father at the age of thirty-two. Parenthood is, to speak philosophically, an absolute ontological shift. Your identity, your orientation in life, your entire being changes. But that's not the point. My point is that I became at parent at the age of *thirty-two*. That means I attended college, graduate school, and served as an ordained pastor of the Evangelical Lutheran Church in America (ELCA) for six years while being married for nearly eight years before begetting a child. At the time, I felt a bit old to be having my first child at *thirty-two*. Incidentally, having my third child two months shy of my thirty-seventh birthday made my thirty-two feel young. Five years of living in a zombie-like state of sleep deprivation ages one quickly. But again, that's not the point.

My point is that I was thirty-two before life and limb changed forever. Prior to having my own children, I had no clue about the constant challenges that befall parents. Take naptime, for example. As a childless pastor at the age of twenty-seven, I thoroughly enjoyed taking Sunday-afternoon naps. Collapsing into the living room recliner and cuddling with an eighteen-pound black cat on my lap, I recovered from the expended energy of my introvert-forced-extrovert morning routine. But when a beleaguered couple with a young baby said to me one Sunday morning, "We are so sorry, Pastor. We haven't been to church in a long while because Charlie's naptime is during worship," I was void of empathy. I was nodding at the couple while they spoke, but my synapses were firing off thoughts like these:

You are telling me that naptime is more important than worship! Really? Unbelievable.

Can't you just shift Charlie's naptime around on Sunday morning?

How hard can it be?

Just do what I do: have naptime after worship.

What a lame excuse for skipping worship!

It's just sleep! Seriously.

It was not my finest pastoral hour. Luckily, I didn't let my mouth echo my mind, though I am sure that sweet couple saw my naïveté oozing out my pores. It is embarrassing to admit my lack of compassion for the parents standing before me.

The irony of my annoyance at these parents, who were actually and amazingly present in worship on that particular Sunday, is not lost on me when I look back now. These days, I seek to atone for the sins of my twenty-seven-year-old naïve self. When those parents sheepishly confessed their absence in worship due to the naptime of their infant, I ought to have responded with grace. Now that I intimately understand the necessity of naptime and the importance of a baby's sleep schedule for the whole family unit, I seek to extend grace to families with young ones:

Wonderful to see you!

Thank you for your presence on this day.

So delightful to have little ones worshipping with us!

I know it is an incredible effort to make it here. We are so grateful.

When you are here, we rejoice!

The smiles and sighs of the parents upon hearing a word of grace and understanding serve as a sign of absolution for me. When conversations with parents of little ones turn to naptime schedules on Sunday morning, I am now quick to say, "Naptime is sacred time, too. We will be here when you can make it"—a much-needed word of grace.

I am convinced that our world needs more grace. Certainly, that includes simple gestures of grace, like the affirmation of the importance of a child's rest on a Sunday morning. But I am speaking of the dire need for the unconditional grace of God that liberates and enlivens hearts, minds, and souls. Our first-born is named Anya Grace. I sometimes think that naming her as we did was our way—albeit subconsciously—of bringing more grace into the world. Her first name, Anya, is a form of Hannah, meaning "gracious" or "God's given gift to the world." Thus Anya Grace means "gracious grace." Or as I like to say, she is our "grace upon grace," a reference to the opening chapter of John's Gospel: "From his [Jesus's] fullness we have all received grace upon grace" (1:16). While we didn't have this passage from John in mind when we named Anya, I'm happy to take credit for the clever afterthought and glad to be reminded of the abundant grace of God whenever I look into her eyes.

Like no other book in the Bible, John's Gospel reminds me of such an abundant grace. The cosmic scene set forth at the outset of John's narrative proclaims, "In the beginning was the Word, and the Word was with God, and the Word was God" (1:1). Then the assertion comes that this divine Word "became flesh and lived among us" (1:14)—and did so as an infant! The radical vulnerability of it all is understood most clearly when you hold a newborn child. Children are a living example of this grace, this sheer gift of God entrusted into our tenuous and flawed hands. It is no wonder God comes to us in the flesh as a baby. Frail and wholly dependent, God incarnates in the Christ-child, claiming our flesh as God's own—holy gift, God-with-us, the Emmanuel we sing of at Christmastime. So to look into your baby's eyes—or your toddler's eyes or your adolescent's eyes or your teenager's eyes—is to see the very eyes of our God. Flesh and blood claimed by God and as God. A gracious grace!

This is the gracious grace we proclaim: God's gift to us most readily seen, smelled, heard, touched, and even tasted in the incarnation of Christ Jesus. Thus proclaims the confession of the Christian church. For two millennia, this consistent and persistent testimony has gathered the church to stand as witness to God's incarnate grace breathing in our world. In every age, the church, flawed though we may be, has proclaimed this grace into a seemingly graceless world. As I write, I think of xenophobia and broken immigration systems, the subversive and deadly systems of oppression, corporate greed, and the unequal distribution of wealth, homeless youth walking the streets, malignant brain tumors, and the heart-wrenching normalcy of mass shootings in the headlines. These represent just a smattering of serious issues that burden bodies and break hearts. Our world craves grace.

As one who clings to hope over despair, I believe all adults yearn to create grace-filled spaces for the youth and children in our world. I felt this acutely in my own body and heart when I became a parent. I suppose that's natural when you cradle an infant whose entire well-being is solely your responsibility. It's a terrifying and marvelous obligation. I think the gift of Christ is the steady reminder that into a world rife with gracelessness,

God's grace is birthed. We are called to be midwives of this grace, creating space where the message of vulnerable love is experienced in all its fullness. This is the testimony of the church—a testimony I understood more intimately when I became a parent. My life, my world, my faith, and my understanding of God's grace all changed when Anya was born.

One thing did not change, however: I continue to believe our God deeply and passionately yearns to grant the world this abundant grace. And amid our flaws and follies, we are all called to share with the world God's grace upon grace upon grace.

+ + +

In 2013, I left my solo call as a parish pastor in Minneapolis to become an associate university pastor at Augsburg University, also in Minneapolis. The atmosphere is dynamic, challenging, and rewarding, to be sure. This shift in call meant a major overhaul of the Sunday-morning routine for our family.

For ten years, every Sunday (and many Saturdays) required me to work. This is no surprise when you go into the ministry in the Christian church. It's what you sign up for, to the dismay of many. But that's the gig. Since the birth of the church, the followers of Jesus gathered on Sunday morning to pray, hear a needed word of God's grace, share in the fruits of the Spirit, and break bread together in the sacrament of Holy Communion. Sunday is the day of Jesus's resurrection, the day when life defeated death. Thus, the church gathers on Sunday to live into this promise.

At Augsburg, however, the university community does not gather on Sunday mornings. Following the academic calendar, we instead worship for twenty minutes every weekday morning and offer a Holy Communion service late on Wednesday night. When class is in session, one can worship on campus six times in one week. This essentially means I have no standing pastoral responsibilities on Sunday mornings. A massive paradigm shift!

My new reality translated into a swift and jarring lesson in parenting in the pew (one of the wooden benches or seats in many church worship spaces) on Sunday mornings.

Allow me to let you in a little secret: it is easier to preach a sermon than it is to sit with small children during worship. Parenting in the pew is hard work. Children wiggle and squirm, cry and throw tantrums, yell and squabble with siblings, and at times defecate while worshipping in the pew. (For a refresher on defecating during worship, see chapter 1, "Poop.") All this happens while the worshipping community gathers to experience the word of God spoken and sung. The tension parents often feel in this setting is real. How do you keep relative order and direct the activity of the kids so that others—you and the family included—may fully enter into worship? It's a daunting task that sadly leaves many parents opting out of worship. Let me say it again: preaching to the pews is significantly easier than parenting from the pews.

Luckily for me, my venture into pew parenting had professional guidance, namely, my spouse. For four years, Melanie alone handled worshipping with our small children. This meant getting one and eventually two little ones up in the morning, fed, ready for worship, to the church building, in the pew, and semi-stationary throughout the worship service. I was always impressed when Melanie, with kids, diaper bag, and activity packs in tow, made it to the church at the outset of the service. Throw in some Minnesota winter gear, and it was quite the sight. Now that I join her in prepping our three children for the Sunday routine, my amazement at her abilities has grown exponentially. Note: I stand in awe of you single parents everywhere who parent day-in and day-out with, at times, little to no support, to say nothing of your participation in worshipping communities!

In my early days of pew parenting, I got in the way more than anything else. Melanie had established a system she executed with an intuitive precision that came only through experience. Coloring books, battery-free toys, and picture books all had their place, effectively timed alongside moments in the liturgy when the kids' participation was more readily observed—messages specifically for children, Holy Communion, sharing of the peace, or the singing of familiar songs. The rhythm she had created for our little family unit on Sundays was like the beat of the drum corps in a high-school marching band. Perfect? Never. Efficient? Always. I, however, joined the parade only to drop the big-ass bass drum onto my feet, trip over the xylophonist in front of me, and tumble into the crowd along the side of the street. When it came to parenting in the pew, I was out of rhythm, two steps behind, and awkwardly trying to claim my new role on Sunday mornings.

Then I discovered the key to Sunday-morning success: *snack*. In truth, it wasn't my discovery. Melanie had used snack for years to establish order among our children in worship. Snack—be it raisins, crackers, dry cereal, or a granola bar—served as the drum major keeping the beat of the morning routine. Often, it was the anticipation of snack that kept the children calm and semi-attentive. At other times, the snack was an all-out bribe. "Hey, if you want snack today, you need to quit pulling your sister's hair and settle down!" Whatever the case, snack was power—a power I was eager to wield, much like a sixteen-year-old drum major blowing a whistle at his classmates in the Fourth of July parade. God bless snacks, and God bless polyester marching-band out-fits and those who wear them!

This wasn't new information to me; snacks had bailed us out in many other settings as well. And of course, parents through-out the generations have learned that if you don't pack a snack on an outing, things can go south in a hurry. Cheerios have been crushed on many church sanctuary floors throughout recent decades for good reason. What *was* new data for me, however, was the way in which, for our children, the worship revolved around snack. The centrality of snack was revealed when my science-oriented spouse made some Pavlovian observations.

To explain, let's start with a quick behavioral psychology lesson courtesy of simplypsychology.org. In the 1890s, Russian physiologist Ivan Pavlov was conducting experiments with dogs and their saliva. That is, Pavlov noted that dogs would begin to salivate when presented with food. The salivating is a hardwired reflex—or in behavioral-psychology terminology, "an unconditioned response" that "required no learning" from an "unconditioned stimulus" (food). While measuring the dogs' saliva output, Pavlov began to notice an increase whenever his lab assistant entered the room. Why? The lab assistant was the one who fed the dogs. Thus, what once was "a neural stimulus" had become associated with an "unconditioned stimulus." The dogs' behavior changed.

Fascinated with this accidental discovery, Pavlov introduced a bell into the feeding practice. Prior to the bell's association with food, the dogs did not salivate when it was rung. Pavlov then rang the bell with each feeding. After some repetition, the bell became a "conditioned stimulus" causing the dogs to salivate. Therefore, Pavlov could remove the food altogether and just ring the bell. The result was a floor covered in slobber.

You can anticipate where I am going with this, can't you? Yes, I am directly comparing my children to slobbering dogs. The snack, as Melanie observed, was the unconditioned stimulus that caused our kids to salivate (or at least get excited). And the conditioned stimulus? Melanie noticed that after settling into the pew on Sunday mornings, a pipe organ prelude would start nearly every worship service. The rich and airy sounds of the organ would serve as the conditioned stimulus for my now slack-jawed, slobbering children. "Can we have snack?" Worship had just begun, as announced beautifully by the organ music, and our kids would fall all over themselves in requesting their snack. Pavlov would be proud!

I don't care how much drool is on the church floor, the prelude is *not* the time to dole out the snack! This is the equivalent to dropping the bass drum in the marching band (I promise, that's my last marching-band reference). If the snack comes out too early, you have relinquished your primary tool to control the kids for the remainder of the liturgy. This I discovered in the early days of my conversion from preacher to pew parent. When the kids are drooling and begging for a snack, you have to use restraint in order to maximize the potential power that a snack provides a parent.

On average, a snack can buy a worshipping adult about seven and a half minutes of relatively low child activity in the pew. Figure more time with raisins and small crackers, less with applesauce pouches and granola bars. My statistical analysis isn't exact, but you get the idea: these are valuable minutes. Throw in a drink, some licking of the fingers (properly sanitized, of course), a little digesting, and you may just have ten solid minutes. You cannot spend these minutes haphazardly at the outset of the worship service; they are best saved for a time when quiet and calm are helpful—during the preacher's sermon, for example. Not only will surrounding worshippers appreciate the effort, the pew parent may also catch the gist of the sermon before it is back to constant motion and an increased likelihood of distraction.

I say all this somewhat playfully, but at the heart of the issue is the truth that pew parenting is hard work. Since worship is a communal time to ascribe worth and honor unto God, parents feel an undue amount of pressure to create or maintain "sacred" space for the sake of the worshipping body—as if sacred means sanitized, silent, and still! I implore you to show me a Bible story of an encounter with God that was silent and still. Too often, we forget that God's presence in our worship can be wild and free, much like the little ones in our midst. We often forget that children, as noisy and distracting as they are at times, can and do lead the way to experiencing the grace of God. I'm not giving up on the importance of snacks in worship to maintain a certain amount of order. Ecclesiastes agrees with me: "For everything there is a season, and a time for every matter under heaven" (3:1). I take this to apply to a time in worship when children's mouths are full and hands are busy. But even when they aren't snacking quietly, my children help me think about and experience the grace of God in new ways. And in this particular case, the new way involves slobber.

Upon further reflection, I now find myself enamored with the idea of my children salivating at the outset of worship. In my mind, it is a testament to the power of ritual practice. True, my kids' motivation in this example is guided more by their taste buds and tummies than anything else. Nevertheless, the Pavlovian association of organ music with snack is a reminder to me of the potential potency of the church's liturgy. At some point, my children will grow older, and the salivating over granola bars at the sound of organ music will stop. The association will no longer be enough to compel them to react in the way they are currently conditioned. What new associations and connections, then, will my children make when we settle into the pew and the organ music warms the sanctuary as worship begins? Will they be salivating at the prospect of hearing the biblical story of resurrection promise? Will they be eagerly drooling in their desire to feel the full welcome of a loving community? Will they be slobbering in anticipation of a taste of God's grace? There's really only one way for me to find out: I'll take them to worship—at this point, still with snack in hand.

+ + +

When I transitioned from preacher to pew parent by way of my new call at Augsburg University, our family had to find a new house of worship to call our own. This, too, is part of the pastoring gig. For the sake of the pastoral office, clergy must step away in order to make space for new leadership. Relationships can be messy, and blurring the boundaries of one's relationship with another person can make things messier. Thus, it is usually a good idea for pastors to move on, even if they remain in the community. This applied to me as well.

In theory, our family could have remained at the church in Minneapolis where I served as solo pastor for four years before being called a seven-minute walk away to the university campus. Our Minneapolis congregation was the only worshipping community my two daughters had come to know in their short lives, and the saints of that small worshipping community loved Anya and Svea dearly. There was great temptation to stay, as Melanie and I deeply valued those relationships and the home our church had become for our girls. In practice, however, it was impossible to remain. Though my Sunday mornings were free for me to worship wherever our family chose, our Minneapolis church was not an option. A new pastor would be called to serve alongside that faith community, and my presence would only hinder the new pastor's relational ministry. A tear-filled leave-taking was had on my final Sunday as their pastor in August 2013 as my heart broke, especially for my daughters.

Finding a church home was a new undertaking for us. The previous worshipping communities we had participated in were predicated on my position on staff. For the first time, we engaged in the practice commonly known as "church shopping." Oh, how I loathe that phrase! It makes church a product of our consumerist culture. The church—the gathered community in Christ—is about meeting the pains and longings of the neighbor and sharing God's grace and love in world. Church is not a product to consume. Of course, I understand the importance of seeking and finding the right church home. Nevertheless, "church shopping" implies that the gospel message is a personal preference, rather than a universal gift. I feel dirty talking about it.

"Church surfing"—that's a phrase I can get behind. Recently, I overheard someone speaking of church surfing as an alternative to the aforementioned practice of seeking a church community. This is a very Holy Spirit–centered approach, and one that calls to mind images of the waters of baptism.

In the sacrament of baptism, while the newly baptized is dripping with the waters of promise, the pastor or priest often marks a sign of the cross upon them, saying something like, "You are sealed with the Holy Spirit and marked with the cross of Christ forever." It is a watery, airy Spirit that claims and empowers the church. To "church surf" is to ride the watery winds of the Spirit from one community to another. The goal is not to find the place that meets *our* needs, but rather to find the community that meets us with a holy and grace-filled welcome offered in tandem with an expectation that we have God-given gifts to share *with the community* for the building up of the body of Christ. In this grace-filled community, we will be strengthened by the promise of Christ to join the church in proclaiming the redemptive word of God in the world.

Our family caught the Spirit's wave, and we washed up on shores on a congregation in a suburb of Minneapolis. To be honest, this congregation was not my first choice at the outset of our church-surfing adventure. It was the obvious choice, to be sure: strong leadership, a social-justice emphasis woven into the fabric of the congregation, excellent worship, financially viable and generous, and close to our house. I assumed this congregation didn't need us; I wanted to go where I perceived we were needed and could readily offer up our gifts. But more importantly, we wanted a place for our children to grow in faith, where they were welcomed, affirmed, and empowered to be the church.

So we church surfed for a while, looking for the community of faith that needed us. It didn't go well. One church near our house excused the children from worship for a learning moment; I refused to be part of a community that communicated clearly to children that their full participation in the liturgy was not expected or welcomed. Another church community, despite our kids banging around in the pews, barely acknowledged our presence. And this was a small church with few kids. They needed us, but they didn't seem to want us. On that day, I had a gut-check moment: I wondered how many times, as a pastor of a congregation, I had failed to adequately acknowledge visitors in the churches I served. Undoubtedly it has happened. That was a painful truth to choke down as our family sat invisible in a small sanctuary that wasn't even half full.

Another faith community close to our home was quite welcoming! The worship was inspiring, the people were kind, the staff was very attentive, and children were fully welcome. It seemed likely we would return with our surfboards and get another feel for the Spirit's movement in that community; however, in speaking to the church leadership, we discovered that the community was not publicly open and affirming of lesbian, gay, bisexual, transgender, or gender-queer persons. Nor was the community ready to engage the conversation. I asked the lead pastor, for whom I have great admiration, if there was a possibility to engage the community in that vital conversation, because that was work I would gladly support—a way in which we could offer our gifts and passions to the community. The answer was no. I heard the sadness in her voice, knowing she wanted it but the congregation was not ready. My heart sank as I knew then and there that we would have to ride the waves elsewhere.

We finally decided to try the obvious church close to our house, even if I felt as if they didn't truly need us. I think we also realized that church surfing is exhausting work. I can now completely relate to families who pack their kids in a car and travel around from community to community, searching for a place of welcome and grace for them. It is tiresome to be the guest all the time; sometimes you just want to go home.

+ + +

Our Minneapolis suburban congregation is not a perfect community. In fact, they confess otherwise, boldly claiming the sinner-saint status we all share. From this vantage point, our church strives "to bear witness to God's 'yes' for the world." When I hear this succinct mission statement, my ears ring with the echo of John's Gospel: "From his [Jesus's] fullness, we have all received grace upon grace" (1:16). This is God's resounding yes, so desperately needed in our grace-starved world: *Yes,* you are made in the image of God. *Yes,* God's promises are for you. *Yes,* you are welcomed just as you are into the community of God. *Yes,* you are God's beloved. God's gracious grace given in Christ Jesus is the *yes* in the flesh!

It wasn't the mission statement that won us over, however. Many congregations have similar sweet-sounding statements. What called us home was the way the mission statement was lived out in the liturgy for us and for our children. Every Sunday morning, worship is set around the table of Holy Communion, the meal of promise—another essential for our family. The arc of the liturgy at our congregation inspires congregational participation through song, prayer, lament, wonder, praise, question, and challenge, following the pattern of gathering, word, meal, and sending. This is an ancient pattern that began to take form among the first Christians, as recorded in the book of Acts: "Day by day, as they spent much time together in the temple, they broke bread at home and ate their food with glad and generous hearts, praising God, and having the goodwill of all the people" (2:46). By experiencing God's yes as a people gathered around grace proclaimed and tasted in the breaking of bread, this community's mission empowers the goodwill of the people, sending us forth from the table to serve in Christ's name. This liturgy becomes a pattern of a living grace worked out by the people of God; it is a shared, embodied endeavor.

This means that children were not just welcomed to be present in worship; they were expected to participate in the whole of the liturgical rhythm with their little bodies. And this became the decisive factor in our "church-surfing" adventure. The necessity of children's full participation was taught and preached by the rostered staff, stated on the website and in their printed materials, affirmed by congregation, and lived out each week. In fact, the worship space itself demands participation by all. And as pastor-turned-pew-parent, I was yearning for such a community.

Our congregation worships in the round, with chairs-like-pews circling around the pulpit and table. As a preacher, I always loved this architectural structure of a sanctuary. A circled community affirmed the centrality of God's grace in the midst of the gathered people—an incarnational, fleshy kind of gathering. As a parent, however, I found this space very disconcerting at first. Practically speaking, worship in the round means everyone can see you. There is absolutely no place to hide when you worship facing each other. If your kids pitch a fit during worship, the whole congregation will not only hear it, but also see it. The reality of fleshy worship can be an unsettling, messy experience for parents who want to sit in the back, close to an exit, with few eyeballs upon them.

In our community's sanctuary, there is no escape; when you enter, you are in the thick of it. The physical space of the sanctuary itself testifies to God's yes for all, because all are seen and known, whether you like it or not. So our kids throw a tantrum, and everyone experiences it with us. It was an unsettling experience at first, but it is part of the fabric of the worshipping body. The culture of the community is informed and shaped by this circular experience, an in-your-face liturgy. This is not to say that we don't look for an exit when a child loses their shit during the sermon, because we do. But, the tantrum is fleshy reality expected and (mostly) graciously received as part of the rhythm of our shared worship. If you welcome children to fully participate in the liturgy, you get the fullness of children, tantrums and tears included.

It takes time to get used to the feeling that your parenting skills—or lack thereof, in my case—are on display for the whole community to see. But there is something nakedly honest in the whole endeavor. I have come to discover the powerful truth of this painfully beautiful experience. When children are fully embraced in worship, parents experience this welcome. It is a word of grace wordlessly spoken. In other words, if children are fully welcomed in worship, that includes their parenting adults, too!

Speaking with parents over the years, I know that worshipping communities haven't always been at their best when welcoming parents and their children. Sadly, I have heard too many stories from parents who have had shaming experiences when trying to worship as family. Side glances and nasty looks have been cast upon many panicking parents trying to soothe or distract rowdy children in the pew. Most parents I know can hastily and astutely read the body language of other adults as they react to their kids. We live in a world of constant judgment and critique, and parents feel plenty judged already, so a glance or a gesture by another adult can send a parent spiraling down the worm-hole of shame and guilt. Given the general atmosphere of critique and criticism parents inhabit on a daily basis, the church has an opportunity to offer a countercultural way of validating and supporting parents and their children. In fact, church is one of the last bastions of genuine intergenerational interaction in our society. This is a gift we ought to celebrate and support. And we need parents—especially parents of young ones—to reflect the fullness of the people of God. Not to mention the fact that children gift us with faith.

But even in a community that constantly and consistently communicates the critical importance and beautiful gift of children in our worshipping body, Melanie and I have had moments where we felt an altogether different message. One Sunday when I was at another church, serving as a guest preacher, Melanie tackled worship at our congregation on her own with the kids. The kids at that time were ages six, four, and one. Melanie, employing all the tricks in her parenting bag (including the snack!), sought to make it through the hour and fifteen-minute worship service. It's never an easy task, but our kids were certainly accustomed to the flow of the liturgy. Still, they are kids. On that particular day, Soren was quite chatty. When a one-year-old gets chatty, it is hard to silence them. But Melanie used her seasoned skills as a pew parent and kept it, as she said, pretty manageable. Melanie and I have developed an innate sense of when to excuse ourselves during worship with a child in tow to tend to some disruption or tantrum or parenting situation. As vital as it is to have children in worship, there are moments when, for the sake of the whole worshipping body, an overly dis-ruptive child needs time and space outside the sanctuary for self-expression. In Melanie's opinion, this chatty moment with Soren was not one of those situations.

Nevertheless, Melanie was approached after worship by an

elderly woman in the congregation. We know this woman and have worshipped with and in proximity to her often over the course of a few years. On that particular day, she said in a very Midwestern, passive-aggressive way, "Maybe it is best for your son to be in the nursery during worship." It was a gut punch to Melanie and, by extension, to me. Melanie was doing everything she could to be present in worship by herself with three small children. And yes, Soren was a little loud that day, but it was nothing that warranted a full-on evacuation of the space. We've had plenty of those moments in our parenting lives, so we understand there is a threshold for distracting behavior. This woman's comment cut deep. What hurt most, I think, was the fact that, week in and week out, we show up with our kids to be part of the community. And this member of the community had experienced our presence often in worship. Her comment became a judgment not just on this day but upon our parenting choices on previous Sundays. It is hard for parents to recover from this kind of critique. And it shows that even in a community fully committed to children in worship, people will still send unwelcome messages with their words and body language.

All the more, I believe that words and gestures of welcome will reiterate the gospel message that all bodies are welcome in the house of God. And that is the power of the liturgical rhythm of the Christian body: it is the fleshy enactment of the grace of God for the sake for the world, a fully embodied experience of the promise of Christ that enables all the gathered to taste and see that God is good. For our worship to be a fully embodied experience, I am convinced that it requires the presence and participation of children. This takes work. Parents and guardians know that sitting in the pews with kids more often than not doesn't feel "worshipful." It can be a disruptive and exhausting endeavor. That's a given truth of parenting, no matter the context. We ought not expect time in worship to be any different—in fact, quite the opposite. The very definition of liturgy is "the work of the people." The rhythm of grace in worship demands our communal work—work we do together for the sake of others. Consequently, the congregation must also publicly and prophetically work to make the welcome of children explicit in word and deed. For I believe that if we see children in our worship, we, as adults, will learn all the more to see God's children in the world. It is ultimately an issue of justice.

There was a moment in worship when I knew without question that our Minneapolis suburban congregation had become home. Months after we officially joined the church community, our children (we only had the two girls at that time) did something in worship: they participated in the dismissal. Since the early church, the liturgy of Christian worship has concluded with a spoken dismissal empowering the people to do the missional work of God in the world. The words differ depending on the season or context of the church, but the typical dismissal is led by the (adult) leader, who says, "Go in peace; serve the Lord"—ancient words calling for new missional acts of mercy and service in the world. The congregation responds to the dismissal in unison: "Thanks be to God."

At our congregation, the dismissal is always led by the children. During the final song or hymn of the service, the rostered leaders of the church invite the children to join them at one of the entrances/exits of the sanctuary. From that location, the children on cue yell, "Go in peace; serve the Lord." The young voices remind us all that our work together in God's world begins again as we exit out into the world. The adults gleefully respond, "Thanks be to God." Children are expected and welcomed all the way through the liturgy and actually are needed for us to know our mission of grace in Christ to serve our neighbors and the world God so dearly loves.

Well, for the longest time, our two girls wouldn't participate in the dismissal. At ages four and two, Anya and Svea found this experience intimidating. Despite our coaxing and the gracious gestures of invitation by the pastors, our girls would not join the cadre of kids in this liturgical practice. But one Sunday morning, long after we had gotten used to their boycotting the dismissal, we lost sight of our kids during the closing song. They must have made a pact, for they decided together to follow the other children to the exit. They ran with a twinge of self-consciousness overcome by their enthusiasm. The liturgy had taken root within them; it was time for them to join the mission. I couldn't hear their voices, and they were probably shocked and uncertain to find themselves leading us in worship at the moment. My guess is they didn't say a word that first time they finally joined the other kids. But my heart burst, knowing they stood with the other dear children of the congregation and reminded us of our mission in Christ.

In that moment, our house of worship became our home.

3. Preachy

vocation (noun): from the Latin word *vocacio*, meaning "call" or "summons"; 1. the understanding that all that we are has been called into being by God, who in turn calls us to love and serve others through our God-given gifts and skills amid our own unique set of circumstances; 2. much, much more than an occupation, but rather, the various ways we live out our faith in our relationships with one another and with God's good creation.

I believe that parents, like pastors, are entitled to be preachy. Preachiness comes with the territory. Now, I am fully aware of the negative connotation that "preachy" has in our vernacular. But that all ends now! I declare that henceforth preachiness is an admirable and desirable quality. How's that for being preachy? As if I have the moral authority and influence to reclaim *preachy* as a word to be seen and experienced in a positive light, I am still going to try. It is a fool's errand, to be sure, but I think my point is worth consideration. Can I get an "amen"?

If you have ever tried to parent a child, you likely have discovered and cultivated your own preachy voice. In those moments of necessary discipline or wide-eyed instruction, the parent preachy voice is a tool to communicate heightened importance demanding immediate attention. There are several types of parental voices that are naturally preachy. (Remember, I am arguing that preachiness is not bad in this scenario.) I believe parents need to get preachy from time to time. There are, of course, parallels between the parent's preachy voice and the pastor's preachy voice, though their efficacy may be different, depending on the setting.

Some parent types use a louder, fuller-sounding voice—shouting. It happens from time to time, though I'm not necessarily condoning it, only naming it. Some preachers I know ramp up their preachy voice while sermonizing and find themselves shouting at their parishioners from the pulpit. This emotive method can be effective for preachers, though probably less so for parents. As a parent, my experience with my own loud preachy voice has been mixed at best. I do garner the attention of my children when I shout, which has been useful in a parking lot or when crossing a busy street. Around the house, however, my shout to break up a verbal or physical altercation between the kids might grab their attention, but it usually bestows fear more than anything else. With the pastor, a shout is less about fear and more about passion. Fear is the overarching interpretative mood my children have experienced when I have shouted, thus clouding my instructional efforts. I have also noted that as my kids get older, they are beginning to respond to my shouting with shouting of their own. A pastor may want her parishioners to shout back at her as sign of shared energy for the gospel message; not so with kids! So, this is not my preferred preachy voice as a parent, though others may find it helpful. I'm not really a sermon shouter either, but I do recognize that it works well for many preachers.

But a parent's loud preachy voice does not need to be a shout; it can be a purposeful elevation or amplification. I often see this done with clenched teeth, but it is probably more effective with a loose jaw, deliberative cadence, and stern tone. So, I might say to my eldest in a louder yet still controlled speaking voice, "Anya. Grace. Lind-Ayres. What. Do. You. Think. You. Are. Doing?" This preachy voice is less about evoking fear and more about communicating the severity of the situation. I employed this voice when Anya was sitting on her tearful sister, trying to wrestle away a book from her. I laud Anya's passion for reading but not her possessive nature regarding her things. My preachy voice set the stage for the "conversation" that followed. I'm pretty sure a time-out followed this very one-sided conversation (I did 98 percent of the talking). That's parenting; that's being preachy! And yes, I have used a similar cadence in the pulpit. I have found it effectively preachy.

One can go in the other direction with one's preachy voice as well. A soft-spoken moment or two in the midst of the sermon does, in this pastor's opinion, go a long way in the preaching task. I'm a proponent of these preachy moments to help focus a point and articulate its importance. When it comes to parenting, however, the method has generally flopped for me. The idea, of course, is that as you get quieter, the kids quiet themselves to listen more closely to what is being said. I have found that my soft, intentional, slightly-above-a-whisper voice is readily ignored by my kids. It might work for others, but this parent reserves the softer voice for the pulpit. It preaches better for me there than in my own home.

As a preacher, I am called to preach but not be preachy. The adjectival form of the word has been associated with lecturing or didactical speaking with a whiff of pretension. So a preachy voice can sound, well, preachy. But as a parent, I find that speaking with my children didactically and with moral authority is necessary for their own well-being as they develop and grow. I suppose the same could to be said of preachers as they speak to their people, though I would tread much, much more lightly in that regard.

As a parent seeking to instruct my children in the faith of Jesus, I have come to own moments when being preachy is precisely my call. I am not speaking strictly of those times to elevate or diminish my voice in order to draw importance to my words. Generally speaking, I can do with fewer of those challenging situations in my parenting life, even if they can be edifying once the dust has settled. Rather, I am of thinking of those preachy moments when the gospel of Jesus's grace, mercy, and love is deeply wedded to our daily living. A preachy moment for me as parent is the time and place when Jesus shows up to strengthen us as a family in the faith to which we are called. And I am convinced that it is my vocation to be a preachy parent. Melanie and I have learned to cultivate these moments in our own ways. Let me and my kids show you what I mean with a few examples of preachy moments.

+ + +

Names are important. The proper names we carefully choose to define and shape our kids, indeed. But equally important, I think, are the nicknames and titles we give our children, born out of love. Melanie and I both adopted our own set of unique names for our children. We did so naturally and without much forethought—or afterthought, for that matter. We just did it. Melanie has called Anya "Sweets," Svea "Babes" ("Baby" was a variation thereof), and Soren "Dooty." These terms of endearment accompany tender moments of expressive love: a welcome-home hug, a kiss goodnight, a midday cuddle on the couch. Sweets, Babes, and Dooty all know their names and feel the significance of their meaning when Melanie addresses them as such.

For whatever reason, I went the vegetable route. "Sweet Potato" (Anya), "Pumpkin" (Svea), and "String Bean" (Soren) all know that when I use their garden names, I do so with care and affection. There have been times when I have mistakenly called Anya "Pumpkin." She is very quick to correct me, saying, "Dad, I'm Sweet Potato." I laugh every time. It is sort of like calling your kid by the pet's name or rattling off all the kids' names until you land on the right one. It happens. I'm always happy to be corrected, particularly when Anya reclaims her own garden name with a sense of pride.

These names are still received well these days. I'll see how they play out when they are teenagers, particularly when they are hanging with their friends: "Hey, String Bean, do you and your friends need anything to eat?" It will be fun to embarrass Soren in that way. Is it bad that I'm already plotting these moments? I guess I see it as a parent's right and responsibility to embarrass their child out of nurturing love; it keeps youth humble.

Names are critically important and define us and our relationships. In the Christian faith, this is most certainly true as well. In the waters of baptism, with God's promise and ordinary water, we are named anew by the grace of Christ Jesus. As part of the baptism rite in my tradition, there is a word of naming. While the newly baptized still drips with the watery promise, the pastor traces a cross on their forehead. This touch of the hand is accompanied by an address to the newly baptized: "*Name of the baptized*, child of God, you have been sealed with the Holy Spirit and marked with the cross of Christ forever." This sign and declaration claims the identity of each and every one baptized into the eternal relationship with our God of love. From that moment on, we walk around with the unseen mark of the cross on our heads, the blessed branding of God's own beloved children.

As a preachy parent, I never want my kids to forget that they belong to God. So I have seized nearly every night as a time to preach their identity to them. And here's the thing: it doesn't take much thought or deep investment of energy, only a few seconds of shared time. Sometimes I think parenting in faith can feel very daunting, sort of like reading the Bible. Where do you even start? In this case, a few brief words and simple action woven into an already ongoing ritual moment in family life is an easy add-on. As I tuck the kids in bed, I get preachy! I make the sign of the cross on their foreheads and say, "Remember you are a child of God, marked with the cross of Christ forever." I timed it. It only takes 4.64 seconds to say—and is worth every hundredth of a second!

I started this preachy moment when Anya was a baby. Naturally, I have continued this practice with the other two. There have been stunning moments in my faith life that have developed because of this five-second ritual. One of my favorites included lying in bed with Svea when she was four. After we had said and sung our prayers together (preachy moments in their own right), I marked Svea's head with word and touch. I remember the night she half closed her eyes as she anticipated her identity as God's own proclaimed once more. With a smile creeping across her lips, she opened her eyes, placed her finger on my head, traced the cross, and reciprocated the blessing: "Dadda, remember you are a child of God, marked with the cross of Christ forever." Svea got preachy with me! She gifted me with the word that named *me* as God's own again; Svea blessed me, strengthened my faith, and renewed my call as her dad. As we smiled at each other in our sacred sharing, I knew this memory would carry me to the end of my days. If I close my eyes, I can still see her four-year-old face radiating God's love onto me.

What made Svea's response all the more significant were the several nights that had preceded that one. There was a period of time when Svea's reaction to this preachy ritual was indignation. She would try to turn away or recoil, saying some variation of "I already know that, Dad." I persisted. Despite her lack of reception, I continued to be preachy and name her as God's. So that evening when she willingly received the blessing and returned it to me, my heart sang. These are the moments we live for as parents—when prayer meets practice, and parenting in faith yields grace and love for all.

It all sounds so sublime, but please don't be fooled. I have struggled many nights in my attempt to offer a blessing. That is, my heart isn't always in it either. Those are nights when I have had enough with the shenanigans and whining and delay tactics and tantrums and blatant ignoring of my instructions. By the time the kids have finally crawled into bed, I have no energy left to be a parent, let alone a preachy parent seeking to cultivate a moment couched in faith. The blessing has still been offered, but I have said these words through clenched teeth, in total desperation, and as an afterthought. There are times when one of the kids might hear the words "Remember you are a child of God, marked with the cross of Christ forever," but what is really said in the tone and tenor of my voice is something akin to "Shut the hell up, and go to sleep!"

Yet the blessing is still offered. The ritual holds us and sustains even when the mood is off, hearts are askew, and words are uttered with false intent. The blessing persists just as surely as God's claim upon us persists. Our identity in Christ's goodness and grace cannot be deterred by our own faults and failings. We are God's own beloved, just as the prophet Isaiah spoke on God's behalf: "Do not fear, for I have redeemed you; I have called you by name, you are mine" (Isaiah 43:1). Our name is clear: beautiful, beloved child of God! We need to hear it every day, and so do the children in our lives. A simple touch accompanied by these or other words spoken on God's behalf are very preachy; I call it parenting in faith, living into the sacred vocation to which God calls us whenever and for whomever we parent. At times, it takes only 4.64 seconds. Not only that, it doesn't even have to be said with a pure heart. God's promise is efficacious for us and, at times, in spite of us!

I recall one night not too long ago, when I was going through the motions of tucking Anya into bed, relying solely on habit and muscle memory. My mind was already drifting to the pile of dishes downstairs and the handful of work emails needing my attention. I was decidedly absent from our nighttime ritual, and as such, I forgot the blessing. As I turned to go to the door, Anya grunted, "Uh, uh, uh," as if she were a baby still learning to how to communicate. I turned around to see her arm was reaching out toward me. She couldn't see me because her nightie-mask—which she *needs* to sleep—was covering her eyes. Slightly irritated because she was speaking weirdly in guttural, baby-like noises, I whisper-shouted, "What, Anya?" Sensing my attention now turned to her, Anya repeated, "Uh, uh." And with her wordless noises, she made the sign of the cross on her own forehead. Her grunts were reminders that I had forgotten to bless her.

Convicted, I felt the irritation slough off my body, and my heart warmed again. With my thumb to her forehead, I reminded her (and me!) of God's name and claim upon us all. The blessing was offered yet again. With a smile and a now very present parenting posture, I said, "Goodnight, Sweet Potato. Love you." For her part, Anya rolled to her side as if to say, "Now I remember who I am; now I can sleep." As I walked back to her door, Anya spoke in a clear, hushed voice, "Love you." Love, serve, and yes, *preach*. This is my vocation as parent in faith, and these moments affirm my call even when I stumble to live into it. Thank God my kids, by way of *their* vocation as children in faith, serve me by preaching and loving me back to my own identity in Christ Jesus.

+ + +

The Lind-Ayres family is not what I would call an accomplished singing household. Neither Melanie nor I sang in choirs growing up, nor have we been vocally trained. We are not strong singers, this is true. But we are faithful ones! Raised in the church, we learned songs of faith from an early age. And as an active churchgoing family, we are grateful to be part of a community that values communal singing and welcomes all our voices.

Despite our lack of technical skill, we still sing to and with our kids. There is power in song, and I think parents often discover this early on with lullabies sung to soothe babies or jingles used to teach them life skills. "Rock-a-Bye Baby," "The Alphabet Song," and the like are tools of the trade for many parents. Words carried on the wings of song can communicate in ways that spoken words simply cannot. So we have chosen to model the importance of song for our kids—even though our singing may be off-key from time to time. The oft-quoted Psalm 100 asserts, "Make a joyful noise to God, all the earth. . . . Come into God's presence with singing." Joy is named; skill is not. What applies to God is applicable to our youth: "Make a joyful noise to children, all you adults, and revel in their presence with singing."

Songs preach. I believe singing to and with children is a tender way to be preachy, to allow Jesus—God's very Word—to show up in the ebb and flow of daily living incarnated in music and song.

In addition to unique vegetable names, I gave each of my kids their own theme song of faith. At some point when each child was nearly the size of a sweet potato or pumpkin, one song among others bubbled up as their own. They all heard faith classics like "Jesus Loves Me" and "This Little Light of Mine" and the Christmas carol "Away in Manger." These songs of faith were often sung while we were snuggling in the rocking chair or when I was bouncing and pacing around the room with them in an attempt to calm them. But at some point, one song landed on each of the kids and, in my mind, became that child's own.

Soren's song is the Appalachian/African gospel spiritual "Down to the River to Pray," popularized in recent years by bluegrass country singer Alison Krauss. The song could be done softly and slowly while clutching a drowsy baby. Or alternatively, the water theme avails itself to a bath time hit: up-tempo and very splashy. For fun, I would replace "brother" in the refrain and sing, "O *Soren*, let's go down, let's go down, come on down. O *Soren*, let's go down, down in the river to pray." He heard this song in many contexts, but generally it has been sung when the two of us are alone. I know Melanie has her own songs that she sings to the kids when I'm not around—special moments between mother and child. "Down to the River to Pray" is our father-son song, and it is about the only song he lets me sing to him. He is quick to shush me if I sing something else; he's a stinker like that.

Karolina Sandell, a nineteenth-century Swedish poet and hymn writer, wrote "Children of the Heavenly Father," and the text was naturally set to a Swedish folk song. Svea, whose name literally means "of Sweden," appropriately received this theme song from me. It is very much a gentle cradle song with the unmistaken theological claim that all children are kept in the loving arms of God. The first stanza reads:

Children of the Heavenly Father,
Safely in His bosom gather.
Nestling bird nor star in heaven
Such a refugee e'er was given.

For Svea's sake, I often changed "Father" to "Mother" and sang, "Safely in *her* bosom gather." I want feminine imagery of God to speak to my girls, so they—and all girls—may rightly see themselves as created in the image of God. I so associated this hymn with Svea that I wrote her baptism-day sermon to this hymn tune, singing portions of it as my message for the day. Partly singing and partly weeping, I proclaimed a message of baptism not just for Svea but for all of us gathered, for we all have our name and identity as beloved children of our heavenly God. What can I say? I got a little preachy on her day!

With our firstborn, Robert Lowry's hymn "My Life Flows On in Endless Song" served as a word of hope and comfort to Anya. Anya announced her colic within hours after recovering from being birthed into the world. We were the room in the birth ward where the crying soundtrack seemed to be on constant repeat. I imagined other new parents walking past our hospital door and wondering if a baby had simply been abandoned in the room. Nonstop crying became our family's existence for the next three and a half months. During this period, Melanie and I rotated sleeping at night in two-hour shifts so the other could handle our crying child. As a result, I found myself in the darkness of night, desperately seeking a way to cease Anya's crying, often singing songs close to her ear so she might hear my voice above her wailing. Given this context, it is no wonder Lowry's hymn became Anya's song. But in truth, the song was just as much for me as it was for her.

The first stanza reads, "My life flows on in endless song; above earth's lamentation, / I catch the sweet, though far-off hymn that hails a new creation." Lowry brilliantly layered the metaphor of song throughout the hymn. Our lives in God are an "endless song" in which we hear God's word as the hymn that creates and recreates us, thus giving us a song to sing as a response unto God. For the refrain proclaims, "No storm can shake my inmost calm while to the Rock I'm clinging. / Since Christ is Lord of heaven and earth, how can I keep from singing?" God sings us into existence, God continues to sing "sweetly" into the world through Jesus Christ, and we can't help but join in the song. And at two in the morning, clutching a colicky child, I needed this song!

The tune is tenderly firm in its proclamation that no storm can shake the calm that comes from Christ alone. For me, the storm was Anya's incessant red-faced screaming. When you feel helpless as a parent and ill equipped to soothe your own child, you begin to question whether you have what it takes to be a parent. I have had real moments of doubting my own vocation as parent. There are times (almost daily!) in my journey that I continue to feel woefully inadequate in my call as parent. Those hard nights with Anya, I needed a word outside myself to break through the raging storm of self-doubt, exhaustion, and sense of helplessness. I needed a word to sing me back to the stable foundation, the rock of Christ Jesus.

So I sang this hymn over and over and over again. Tears streaming down Anya's beet-red face and welling up from my blood-red eyes, I sang to her, to me, and to God—a prayer in the long night. Usually her crying raged on through the song, but there were fleeting moments when the colic spell was broken. She would look at me in an all-too-brief moment of calm, and I would feel my call as parent being restored anew. The question "How can I keep from singing?" became my sung refrain, even when I didn't feel like humming a tune, let alone singing one.

Anya now is learning piano. As much as I yearn to hear songs of faith played by her, I welcome any music that fills the house. I rejoiced upon hearing a nearly flawless beginner's version of Bobby Day's "Rockin' Robin." Anya did learn a simple version of the familiar hymn "Amazing Grace" and played it at one of her early recitals. It was gorgeous. As she practiced, I sang along with her from time to time. These are the preachy moments I savor as we preach God's word to each other. As much as I try to not be overbearing with faith and to allow God moments to naturally occur within the rhythms of our family life, I am plotting a particular request. When Anya is ready, I will ask her to learn "My Life Flows On in Endless Song." My special ask will include a retelling of its importance to me—my theme song for her from the earliest of days. If she accepts my request, as I pray she will, I anticipate putting out a box of tissues somewhere near the piano—or at least, somewhere near me. Because this parent is going to lose his shit, becoming a nearly unrecognizable puddle-of-a-mess-of-Dad. And that's okay; children preaching the faith to us in word and song have that kind of power.

+ + +

At the age of fifteen, I had an inkling that I would become a preacher. Actually, as I ponder the events of one summer night over a quarter century ago, "inkling" falls woefully short. That moment in my life demands a heavier word, a more spiritually charged word. *Epiphany* or *revelation* may be more accurate to my experience. These words seem better equipped to convey the weight of what happened to me. How else do you describe the moment when a starlit walk was interrupted by the voice of God?

Let me be clear: I am not prone to hearing voices. In fact, it has happened to me just this once. Because it was a one-time event, I sometimes wonder if it was something more akin to a waking dream or hallucination spurred on by an adrenaline-induced imagination. The default response to a supernatural experience in our modern era tends to be skepticism fueled by an unwavering commitment to rationalism. One result of this cultural mind-set, I believe, is the squelching of the revelatory activity of God. Put another way, if you admit to hearing the voice of God, you may be labeled "questionable of mind." At fifteen, I was well attuned to this fear and kept my revelation quite private.

Yet I believe there is room in our world where we can encounter God with the fullness of our senses. I wonder whether can we still see a divine vision or hear a divine call as described over and over in the holy Scriptures. Moses saw a burning bush and heard God speak from the flame (Exodus 3); the young boy Samuel heard God speak his name three times (1 Samuel 3); Ezekiel had a vision of bones come to life (Ezekiel 37); Mary the mother of Jesus saw and spoke to an angel, while nine months later, the shepherds saw the night sky burst with the sights and sounds of an angelic chorus announcing Jesus's birth (Luke 1–2); Mary Magdalene encountered the resurrected Jesus in the garden (John 20); the apostle Paul was blinded by the light of heaven during his conversion on the road to Damascus (Acts

9). And an acne-rich fifteen-year-old in Fergus Falls, Minnesota, heard the voice of God on a late-night summer walk home.

I do believe I heard the voice of God, though I am extremely hesitant to tell people. My hesitancy, given that my profession is to *speak* about God, is admittedly ironic. Even when people ask directly about "my call" to be a pastor, I speak in generalities about "feeling" the call or "just knowing" when I was a sophomore in high school. Almost never do I share the details of that night some twenty-five years ago. I know we live in a cultural context that readily dismisses or diagnoses voices in one's own head. At the time, I was also aware that adolescents are not often taken seriously when it comes to matters of faith. The church (and really society at large) has not been faithful in affirming the gifts of youth and young adults among us. I felt all of these cultural forces enough to know I'd best keep my revelation to myself.

Another reason I kept my God-encounter private has much to do with my personality. My modus operandi is deflection. I avoid making the topic of any conversation about me or drawing attention to myself. My Midwestern sensibilities will do anything to sidestep comments or compliments aimed in my direction. Don't get me wrong; my ego can feed off praise and affirmation like a sewer rat in a trash can. Those human impulses are just that—human. I have them aplenty! But I truly believe that humility is a virtue, a virtue I seek to cultivate.

So I submit my God-call story in humility because it is inextricably linked to how I understand myself as a parent. That is, my sense of vocation shaped through my childhood encounter with God has become the interpretative lens for my vocation to parent and raise children in the faith. My call to be a preacher and my living out of that call have shaped my understanding of parenthood and the sacred call to live out my faith as a dad. So I share in these pages this story from my own youth, when God was doing a new thing in my life, because the call is still working in my life years later as I have become a seasoned preacher and one seeking to parent in faith.

Though I have questioned, ignored, doubted, and challenged my experience at various times since, I am convinced that in late June 1993, God called me to preach and be a pastor in Christ's church. As I said, I heard the voice of God. And this is true, but the voice of God was more than an auditory experience. What I felt was a full-bodied experience. It wasn't a ringing in my ears but a reverberation throughout the whole of my body. It was as if the voice came from within myself but I knew that it was not my own. In short, I was overcome by the divine.

It was one of those cloudless nights when the midnight sky gaped open before me and the stars owned the earth. I had been playing basketball with a handful of friends at Jake's house, some two miles from my home. We had lowered the basketball hoops in Jake's driveway to nine and a half feet; for that reason, our two-versus-two games were punctuated by the rattling of the rims as we became gods, our feet hovering off the ground as we clung to the orange-painted circle of metal. The invincibility of our teen years was yet to be dashed as we sweated and hollered and laughed while the stars watched, waiting.

I was the youngest in the group, with my sixteenth birthday still weeks away. As our games came to a close, with our curfews beckoning us home, my friends were piling into cars they were able to drive. But the night and God were not done with me. Something stirred in me that manifested itself as an irresistible impulse to walk home. As I started down the road, my friends were cajoling me to hop into one of their cars. I declined their offers, compelled by what I now understand was a prelude to the call from God. My dear friend Marc, who these days, along with his wife Kari, is the baptismal sponsor to two of my kids, even pulled his car over and said, "Justin, get in." I couldn't explain it in that moment—and still struggle—but I knew I had to make that journey. Being assured that I was okay, Marc reluctantly drove away, leaving his friend to encounter God.

Minutes later, God spoke to me, setting me on a path of living into this wild call to preach about Jesus's love. I heard and felt just a handful of words within me: "Pastor. Serve. Preach. Love." The full-bodied experience I had with God reverberated to the core of my being. In that precise moment, as the stars sang the night's praise, I remember my mind succumbed to awe while my body trembled with giddiness, utter joy. It felt glorious to be in God's own presence, and I imagine my countenance was beaming nearly as bright as those stars lighting the path. Praise reflecting outward, mirroring a heart kindled by this divine call: pastor, serve, preach, love.

During the rest of the journey homeward, my senses were crackling, fully awakened to the night's mysteries. My mind was flooding with thoughts of a future, unknown yet certain. Pastor. Me, a pastor? Serving, preaching, loving in God's name? Indeed! I heard it and felt it in my inward self. Sleep was in short supply that night, as my heartbeat set a pace that rest could not over-take. God had spoken to me—me, a fifteen-year-old kid in small-town Minnesota on the outskirts of town. I knew this to be true. But now what? After some consideration, I did what any overly self-conscious teen would have done: I kept it a secret. That sum-mer, I told only my trusted neighbor and friend Mike. But over time, the circle of trust widened as I began to test the spirits and wrestle with my vocation: pastor, serve, preach, love.

I share my epiphany/revelation/call story here for several rea-sons. For starters, I want to remind us all that children and youth are witnesses to the living God and serve as leaders in our jour-ney of faith—not just in the future, but now, today! I myself, as an adolescent, had an impactful experience of God in Christ Jesus and felt I was uniquely poised to offer something to the church. There are children and youth in our midst seeking space to testify to their own faith in God. Our younger believers are looking for a people and a place to wholly welcome their own wrestling with God and God's call upon their lives. Our call is to provide nurturing households and supportive communities of faith for the pint-size spiritual guides in our lives. Our task is not to dole out answers but to hold their questions and wonder with them about God's expansive love and unconditional grace.

Tending to my call story also enables me to look for God at work in the many kids who bless my life. It is all too easy to go through the motions of daily living and fail to recognize that God is up to new things in and through the lives of my own children and the children I am fortunate to interact with as uncle, neighbor, community member, teacher, and friend. God tugged on my heart at the age of fifteen, but God called, gathered, enlightened, and strengthened me well before that summer night of vocational eruption. My own faith and call demand sensitivity to God at work in the little ones among us. The more I remember this truth and am cognizant of the Spirit's tendency to transcend age, the more I see God alive in the faith of children. Attention to the budding and blooming faith of children is what keeps my own faith active and alive. It becomes an anticipatory practice, if not an addictive one: to watch and to listen to the wild testimonies of kids as they preach and teach about God—good stuff, the best stuff.

And finally, the most important reason I share my call has everything to do with you. I believe with my whole body that God speaks to us. Sometimes God uses a personal experience that excites the senses; other times, God speaks to us through the actions and examples of others. The call that God placed upon me to preach is, ultimately, about others—about you! God said to me, "Pastor. Serve. Preach. Love." So, my call story itself is a sermon to preach to you this truth: the God who is calling me is the God who is also calling you. You, too, have a vocation—many vocations, in fact. Maybe not "pastor" in the professional sense of the word, I'll give you that. But what about service? How is God calling you to serve the neighbor? What about preach? What is God calling you to say and proclaim in your daily living? Trust me; you don't have to be a pastor to preach. We preach with our lives. What about love? Where is God calling you to share love with others? These calls are not restricted to the public profession of pastor. Thank God! These are vocational words of a living faith borne out in the world. These words from God to me are God's words to you as well. They are our vocations—our callings—as people of faith.

When I heard the voice of God, God spoke within my body as an affirmation of who I am as a child of God. This is the birthright of faith for all of us, gifted by God and affirmed in the promise of holy baptism. For me, the "pastor" call was particular to my profession. But really, it was just one of the avenues God was calling me to live out this birthright and baptismal witness: to serve, to preach, and to love. God summons us all with our various gifts and skills amid our own unique set of circumstances. We live our lives following the summons.

Parent. Serve. Preach. Love. This is the call. At the age of fifteen, I heard God say "pastor" and followed that path. But since that summer day decades ago, I have learned that the vocation of a living faith is embracing all the ways we are called to use our hands and hearts in service to the gospel of Jesus. The divine call commands me to be nothing short of preachy—to serve in trust and proclaim in love the grace and mercy and joy of our God. As a pastor, yes, but more so, as a parent. For me, there is no call more critical than that of parent. The children in our lives are ours to love and serve. Damn, it is hard work, and I fail constantly. But the call is clear: "You shall love the Lord your God with all your heart, and with all your soul, and with all your might. Keep these words that I am commanding you today in your heart. Recite them to your children and talk about them when you are at home and when you are away, when you lie down and when your rise" (Deuteronomy 6:5–7). In the ebb and flow of parenting, we are presented with moments to teach the faith gifted to us by God, to show the unconditional love of Christ, and to sing in trust of the Spirit's power at work in the world.

Thus, I am writing and reflecting about parenting *in faith*. Faith is a vital component of this whole endeavor. I pray God gifts you and me with the faith to believe my feeble words. But mostly, I pray that we believe God's own call upon our lives. And whether or not you have children (or grandchildren or nieces or nephews) of your own, I believe God calls us *all* to parent the children and youth in the many and various communities we inhabit. So really, the vocational impulse from God that matters most might be this: *Parent*. Serve. Preach. Love. This vocation, this summons, this calling is precisely where faithfulness in Christ is manifest in word and deed. In other words, God calls us to get preachy and parent in faith, reciting and enacting with the children in our lives this most blessed truth: we are all God's beloved children, now and forever.

4. Maundy Thursday

Maundy Thursday (noun): from the Latin *mandatum*, meaning "command" or "mandate"; 1. the day of Holy Week (Thursday) when at his Last Supper, while washing his disciples' feet, Jesus gave his *mandatum* to "love one another as I have loved you" (John 13:31); 2. the beginning of the Great Three Days (Maundy Thursday, Good Friday, the Vigil of Easter), which mark Jesus's passion and lead, ultimately, to Easter resurrection; 3. the night in which Jesus was betrayed.

Anencephaly. That's a medical term I will not soon forget.

In the spring of 2008, we lived childless in Clarkston, Georgia, an inner suburb of Atlanta. Near her completion of medical school in Minnesota, Melanie was "matched" at Emory University's pediatric residency program. Match Day is a strange ritual practice in the medical world. On one particular day in the final semester of medical school, students all across the country find out simultaneously where they are going to continue their medical education and practice. The "match" is made between the students and the programs where they have applied. Melanie ranked her top six pediatric programs, and those programs ranked her. Presumably, these rankings—along with rankings of all programs and medical students—were entered into some complicated computer algorithm, and "matches" were spit out. I imagine an archaic dot-matrix printer kicking out an unending scroll of paper in some basement lab at an undisclosed location, the printing head moving back and forth horizontally to the loud signature sound of printers of the 1980s: *zeet-zeet-zeet*. It will not shock you to know that I have absolutely no idea how the mechanics of Match Day really work. There is an air of mystery to the whole ordeal.

What I can tell you is that in March 2006, family and friends gathered with the entire graduating medical-school class of the U of M to find out the results of the match. There was a palpable and exceedingly anxious energy in the room. Hors d'oeuvres were served as medical students mingled with one eye constantly on the clock. At the appointed time, a brief program began. Words long forgotten were spoken by a medical-school faculty member or two to mark the occasion. All that mattered were the envelopes.

Like holy artifacts shrouded in mystery and emanating a power beyond themselves, 216 white envelopes were laid out on a table. The contents within dictated the trajectory of the lives of all who filled that banquet hall. I don't recall how the envelopes made it into the hands of each medical student, but strict instructions were given to wait until everyone had their own. Then the command to open was delivered. It was a bizarre communal experience that felt like a cross between the Oscars and the lottery, though the envelopes weren't nearly as elaborate, nor the prize as lucrative. Shouts of joy mixed with tears of sadness—an array of emotion on public display as classmates either consoled or congratulated one another, and in some cases, did both. Melanie's letter read Emory University School of Medicine, Atlanta, Georgia. It was time to start packing.

Our move to the Atlanta area in the summer of 2006 meant leaving my first congregation in Saint Paul, where I had served as the associate pastor for three years. Saying goodbye to the lovely people where I first took on the title of "pastor" was difficult, but we were ready for a new adventure. Shortly after we moved down South, I received a call to serve as the associate pastor of a church in a northern suburb of Atlanta. We lived much closer to Atlanta proper, so the commute from our house to the church was forty-nine minutes, minus the heinous Atlanta traffic. Many sermons were crafted in my mind while I was stuck seemingly hours on end on I-285. But the incredible staff of the church and the hospitality and mission of the congregation members made every minute worthwhile. I needed this community much more than they needed me, and that became all the more evident in the spring of 2008.

Melanie and I had been married for nearly seven years, with a focus on establishing our professions. At that time, however, we believed we were ready to be parents. It was hilarious, really. I don't think anyone can ever be *ready* for the radical overhaul of one's life that a child necessitates. But bodies, hearts, and minds lull those called to be parents into believing that readiness is possible. *Openness* to being a parent is probably more accurate than the illusory idea of readiness. We were open.

Sometime in January 2008, Melanie and I watched a pregnancy stick as if it dared us to a staring contest. Blinkless moments passed until we saw it: a pink line. Positive. We were caught in a mixing bowl of immediate emotions—joy stirred together with disbelief folded into gratitude, garnished with wonderment. I can summarize it best in one phrase: Holy shit! It's a surreal moment whenever hope and reality kiss—in this instance, kiss on a stick. We figured a child in Melanie's final year of her pediatric residency would be as good a time as any to tackle this parenthood venture together. The plan was in motion, or so we thought.

Living some 1,100 miles from family in the Midwest made keeping the news secret quite easy. We wanted to maintain secrecy until we were safely out of the first trimester, but bodies can unconsciously betray the emotions we seek to keep in check. In fact, my senior colleague at our north-of-Atlanta church took one look at me the day following the pregnancy test and knew. So much for playing it cool.

The Rev. Dr. Paul W. Baumgartner had served a Lutheran congregation in Savannah, Georgia, for quite some time before he came to the Atlanta area. He was a born and bred Southerner whose accent, though not thick, was heavy enough to provide an old-world gravitas to his words spoken from the pulpit—or from anyplace, for that matter. His parents appropriately named him after the apostle Paul (Paul's father was a Lutheran pastor as well), for Paul W. has been a living interpretation of the apostle's words, "For I am convinced that neither death, nor life, nor angels, nor rulers, nor things present, nor things to come, nor powers, nor height, nor depth, nor anything else in all creation, will be able to separate us from the love of God in Christ our Lord" (Romans 8:39). Paul W. has shown me and countless others what this unconditional love looks like in word and deed. It is the W, however, that is perhaps the most fitting part of his name. His W is the initial for Wisdom. Paul Wisdom is a tall order of a name to live up to, but somehow he has done it—wise pastor, strong preacher, insightful counselor, kind mentor, and dear friend. After learning about the pregnancy, I sat in Paul Wisdom's office for one of our regular meetings, when Paul looked me up and down and asked, "Is Melanie pregnant?" The body will betray you if you are not careful. And all the care you can muster to stave off your body's betrayal may not be enough.

After Melanie had the official pregnancy test at the clinic, she scheduled her first ultrasound during Holy Week, the busiest week of a pastor's life. That was irrelevant to me; I could feel my priorities shifting already. Perhaps this priority realignment was the equivalent to my own Braxton Hicks contractions getting me ready for the real thing. I could feel things changing. The appointment, I believe, was on Monday of Holy Week, which would make sense, because I typically reserved Mondays as my day off from non-emergency pastoral duties during the week. To be honest, though, parts of that week are a blur, yet other moments are disturbingly clear, as memory's grip exerts its fierce hold when and where it wishes.

For instance, I remember that the ultrasound tech was friendly and chatty as she kindly reflected our excitement back to us upon learning that this was our first baby. As Melanie climbed into the exam chair, I found the roller chair designated for the supportive partner. I remember not knowing where exactly to position the chair or what to do with my hands—a foretaste of the feelings of helplessness I often had during the birthing process. The ultrasound began.

Despite all the technology at work, an ultrasound has a primordial quality to it; the sounds are muffled, like words spoken while submerged underwater. Perhaps creation described in Genesis was God's first ultrasound—the womb of the universe muffling God's voice calling forth life as "darkness covered the face of the deep while a wind from God swept over the face of the waters" (Genesis 1:1). The tech moved the ultrasound paddle around on Melanie's belly with skill and precision. I saw blobs and strange shapes telescoping in and out, unable to discern what I was viewing. Being in the medical field, Melanie was able to read the monitor, despite it being outside the realm of her specialty. With guidance from the medical folk in the room, I began to see limbs, the torso, and the beginning of facial features. The tech kept up her chatter as she pointed out the newly forming terrain of our child's body. And God said, "Let there be a baby," and there was a baby being created before our technologically enhanced eyes.

The heart monitor was turned on, and the tech declared, "A very healthy heartbeat." My idle hands reached for Melanie's. The beating of the baby's heart added yet another layer of reality stacked upon all the others. This was happening, really.

Suddenly, the vociferous tech became reticent and intent on the monitor, which revealed a particular angle of the baby's head. Melanie watched for a moment and then asked, "Does the baby's head look a little weird to you?" Silence. Caught up in the moment, I didn't think too much of the tech's newfound introversion. But Melanie's question undeniably hung in the air with nowhere to land. As the appointment came to a quiet close, the tech printed a few pictures from the ultrasound, escorted us to the lobby, and said, "The doctor will be ready for you in a few minutes," or something to that effect. She said it in a way that felt like a normal ebb and flow of this type of appointment, but we began to wonder as we waited.

After a healthy interval, we were called into an OB/GYN's office and asked to sit. We were still clutching the photos from the appointment. Formalities were exchanged, but the doctor wasted no time. She said, "It appears the fetus has anencephaly." Under different circumstances, I might have recognized the Greek etymology of the word, given my college and seminary training in the language, and parsed it out: *an* = no; *en* = in; *cephala* = head; "no in-head."

Anencephaly. A chasm opened in my stomach, a dark pit of anxiety. Whatever she had to say following that word wasn't going to be good. Hence the silence of the dutiful tech, the long and unusual wait post-exam, and a special sit-down visit in the leather chairs in the doctor's office. She continued, "The fetus's brain and skull are not growing normally, and actually you can see there is no cranium. It is a neural-tube defect." Melanie had seen it, the tech understandably had hidden it, and now the doctor was explaining it. "I'm sorry. The pregnancy is not viable."

Tears began streaking down my face, creating two wet-warm paths from eye to jaw. If given the choice, I prefer not to weep in the presence of strangers. But we know all too well the body's ability to ignore particular wants and wishes of the mind. Another betrayal? Perhaps. But in that office at that particular moment, I didn't give a shit. And if I had, it wouldn't have mattered. My body summoned tears, a grief offering to physically mark that painful moment in our lives.

At this point, I don't remember much more of the day or days that immediately followed the gut-wrenching news. The jarring turn from joy to woe sent me into a tailspin. I know Melanie and I cried in that office for a bit before following the OB/GYN's direction to schedule a more comprehensive ultrasound with a specialist. We went to that appointment only to hear again what we already knew. If brought to term, our baby would not have a cranium and would not survive long outside the womb. No in-head. No major portion of the brain. No cranium. No top skull or scalp. Anencephaly. Still, the heartbeat remained healthy and strong, an eerie juxtaposition of the tenacity of life in the face of imminent death. Given the circumstances, Melanie was promptly scheduled for a dilation and curettage (D&C) to remove the fetus and terminate the pregnancy. The procedure was set for that Thursday—Maundy Thursday of Holy Week.

The holes in my memory of those two days waiting for the procedure are gaping, as grief claimed its keep. I do recall a few things, however. Like how the ultrasound photos moved around the kitchen, marking the previous spot where one of us had spent time weeping over this dying dream. Or the call I made to my mother to tell her the news that Melanie was pregnant and—in the same breath, as a screech of joy came from her end of the phone—to stumble over the word *anencephaly*. Or how strong Melanie was to keep on with her work while carrying this weight in her body.

My colleagues, the Rev. Dr. Paul W. and Deacon Michelle Angalet, were beyond incredible. We had three worship services on Maundy Thursday, and clearly I was going to miss them. Without blinking, they told me not to worry about it. On that Wednesday, the three of us staff members gathered in Paul's office as they shared tears with me, prayed for Melanie and the baby, laid hands on me, and then lovingly blessed two hand-knit blankets made by the "Yarn Angels" of the congregation.

An extraordinary ministry of tender care, the Yarn Angels was a group of mostly women who gathered monthly to knit blankets to share with people in times of joy and sorrow. In fact, they weren't blankets but prayer shawls created as a visible sign to wrap the recipient in love and hold them in prayer. I had been on the giving end several times, having made pastoral visits with a prayer shawl in hand. Receiving these prayer shawls was a humbling and holy moment, a grace gift. Today, some years later, these prayer shawls sit on our couch in the basement, where our three children snuggle with them or use them to build a blanket fort. The prayers continue to hold us!

At the time Melanie was prepped for the D&C procedure, she told me she was ready to have it done. I cannot fathom the endurance it takes to walk around with a beating heart in your belly, knowing that it will inevitably and necessarily be silenced. As I reflect on those days, I am again amazed at her stamina, her courage, her grace. That Maundy Thursday morning, I recall, I grasped Melanie's hand on the hospital bed/gurney as she was about to be wheeled into the operating room. My eyes watering to capacity, I offered God a silent, heart-held prayer as the hospital staff shuffled around us. We looked at each other and allowed the prayer to move through our bodies with a squeeze of the hand. Melanie had steeled her resolve and flashed a smile to assure her weepy husband that it would be okay. It was time for Melanie and baby to go. I often feel helpless in this world, but perhaps no more than when a loved one—and in this case, two—is being wheeled away for surgery.

We call them "waiting rooms" in hospitals and clinics, but I really experience them as prayer chapels. No matter one's faith or nonfaith, the helpless feeling that accompanies waiting becomes an invitation to entrust our fears and desires to God. There is a heavy energy in waiting rooms that crackles with prayer. Having spent considerable time in these makeshift prayer chapels with families as their pastor sharing in the feeling of helplessness, I have become attuned to feeling the prayer energy. It is a lot to bear, so it is only natural to crave mindless distractions to carry us through. Wall-mounted TVs, cell phones, books, games, and tentative conversations with others all become tools to distract. But the prayers punctuate it all.

I sat alone at a small table, picking at a blueberry muffin while nursing a tepid cup of coffee. Futilely trying to read some theological article, I mostly stared at the hospital pager assigned to me. The light blinked every few seconds, assuring me it worked, but it didn't ease my trust in the technology as time passed. This certainly wasn't the hospital moment I had envisioned for us when that pregnancy stick flashed its pink line. After several minutes blurred and countless prayers muttered, I was startled by the OB/GYN doctor who found me in the waiting room. Her head cover still in place and surgical mask around her neck, she joined me at the table—an answer to my prayers.

Impressed that she took time to seek me out without the assistance of the pager, I listened to her synopsis of the procedure. A cloud of words descended upon me; reaching out, I held onto the ones that mattered: "smooth," "good," "recovery," "home." Sadly, this was a routine for her, but she did it with the care and attention of a doctor who knows the heartache she holds in her surgical hands. She informed me that it would be another forty minutes or so as Melanie recovered before I could see her. Gently touching my hand, she then said, "I know you will be good to her." Those parting words, a benediction of sorts, empowered me anew to live into my promise to care for Melanie in sickness and in health. We both were sick, of course; the loss of a baby was an open wound in our heart. But it was Melanie's body that bore the physiological sickness as she recovered in post-op.

Jumbled memory and an intensity of emotion have left me

with little recollection of the moments of getting Melanie from hospital to home. I know a wheelchair was involved with gentle assistance into our black Toyota Corolla as I sought to over-function in my quest to be good to her. By the later afternoon hours on Maundy Thursday, we were back home, with Melanie resting in bed. While I anxiously (and I hope tenderly) fussed over my wife—the comfort and care of her body—the body of Christ was gathering to mark the day Jesus gave his mandate "to love another as I have loved you." And I was at home, where I needed to be.

+ + +

I have a deep love for the Gospel of John, so I can't help but note its centrality within the Maundy Thursday liturgy. The thirteenth chapter of John is the focal text of the day's worship, as Jesus, with basin and towel, gives his *mandatum* in the washing of the disciples' feet. It is a love act, a sign of heavenly hospitality accompanied by a commandment of charity unto others. While I was at the hospital and then at home with Melanie, supporting her recovery, my congregation gathered to reenact this act of service and hospitality—washing one another's feet and remembering Jesus's words. All of this happens within the context of Jesus's final meal as the shadow of Judas's betrayal looms large.

The drama of Jesus's passion begins in the Gospel of John as the body of Christ gathers and hears, "Now before the festival of the Passover, Jesus knew that his hour had come to depart from this world and go to the Father. Having loved his own who were in the world, he loved them to the end" (John 13:1). The departure of Jesus—namely, his betrayal on Maundy Thursday and subsequent death on the cross on Good Friday—is definitive. Jesus loved them "to the end."

As a pastor, I have tried (and no doubt failed) to teach children and youth why Good Friday is called "good." Defining Jesus's bloody suffering and excruciating death as anything but *bad* is a hard sell. Because let's be clear: what humanity (we) did to Jesus on the cross at Golgotha was God-awful. Yet it is the place where God's salvation is at work—not because suffering is good, but because God is good. I believe the cross of Christ saves because that is where God shows up.

In the deepest of suffering, amid all shame while gasping in the throes of death, God's self-sacrificing love is revealed in fullness. God loves us to the end! In spite of the gruesome suffering and agony, God's love prevails. Sin and death are met in the body of God. At the foot of the cross, we see the full extent of God's passion for us. A God that knows the depth of human suffering knows the depths of us! Was it a good day? No. And yes.

I have clung to this promise as I have pastored people in their deep suffering when our human brokenness unto death has overwhelmed. I have prayed with people, "God of goodness and love, show up *again* in this hour of need." And I have clung to this promise in my own brokenness and heartache when words like *anencephaly* have sent me spiraling into suffering's firm grip. The cross of Christ is, for me, the assurance that God will persist in loving us at all times. And this is the fullness of God's passion proclaimed on Maundy Thursday into Good Friday and all the way to the sun's rising on Easter morning.

The story of the totality of God's love known in the cross and empty tomb shapes the entire story—your story and mine. Divine love outpoured is our story's middle and beginning because it is ultimately our end, for God is our end. Even in suffering, the ending is clear and true. Does this nullify our suffering? Hell, no! It legitimizes our suffering as known, seen, and experienced by God's own self. God goes with us into our heartbreak and into our pain with a decisive promise: I love you and will never let you go. It is a heavenly welcome mandated by an earthly act: "Love one another as I have loved you" (John 13:31). I am convinced that this love saves, tomorrow, today, and to the end.

I am convinced that nothing can withstand this divine love—not even anencephaly.

+ + +

Though I missed Maundy Thursday worship the day of Melanie's D&C, I experienced Jesus's mandate of love in the days and weeks that followed. I would like to think that I was a living testament to faith and love in Christ in the face of suffering and death, to think that in those tender days I believed and completely trusted that God's promise held Melanie, held me, and held our unborn and now-terminated fetus. That simply is not true. Pain and heartache rattle faith, as they have every right to do. Why else would the book of faith include Psalm 22, which begins, "My God, my God, why have you forsaken me?" We are granted permission to doubt and question and challenge God, especially in the darkest nights of the soul. Jesus did so as he hung on the cross; ought it not be expected of us as well?

I did not take up the Psalmist's cry, however. I did not feel forsaken by our experience of anencephaly—that much I know. My faith was not gone; it simply was not enough. My personal faith was unable to sustain the heft of grief I felt at the loss of the pregnancy. I relied on Melanie, I relied on our family and friends, and I relied on the congregation. In short, it was the communal faith that upheld my wavering personal faith.

Without hesitation, I will assert to my dying day that God does not seek to teach us lessons through suffering, as if God is some vindictive schoolteacher. But I do believe we learn in these circumstances nonetheless. Or maybe it is more accurate to say that I believe God's love is present in suffering, and it is variations of this truth that we learn in our trials. I learned (again!) that my faith relies on the faith of others. God did not seek to teach me this lesson by causing pain; rather, I learned that God was present through others who entered into our pain and cradled us in care. This is the saving communal faith expressed in love that "bears all things, believes all things, hopes all things, endures all things" (1 Corinthians 13:7), especially when one's individual faith falls short.

That year, following Maundy Thursday, Good Friday, and the Vigil of Easter—the journey from betrayal through suffering and cross into the mystery of resurrection—Easter came. It always does, thanks be to God! But that year, I was Eastered by the love acts of others. Resurrection took the shape of the body of Christ that chose to enter into our sorrow. For with our permission, the prayers offered that Easter Sunday contained a petition for Melanie and me at the loss of our unborn fetus. As this truth was named publicly within the worshipping body, people responded. During the intervals between the four worship services on that Easter Sunday, a line of people stood outside my office door. No joke! The people of God were literally lined up to be present to me in my suffering. Another lesson learned: sometimes the pastor of a community needs to be pastored by the community.

With hugs and tears, the community of God's faithful met me in my grief. By naming aloud the truth of our pregnancy lost, the liturgy gave permission for the community to talk about this kind of suffering. Sadly, issues surrounding pregnancy, loss, and fertility are often silenced by our culture, the church included. It's all the more reason to publicly name and claim the issues that weigh our bodies down with grief and undue guilt. Too often, people suffer silently, and the church is called to do a better job of bringing painful issues out into the light of day so we can bear all things together through God's incarnate love. I am grateful that Easter happened on that Sunday, as we publicly shone light on this issue, making it known to the whole body.

The people in the line outside my door had tragic stories to share. As people held me in their loving embrace, they named their own stories of hurt and heartache. One sweet couple in their sixties spoke about the stillborn death of their child. They had learned that the child Susan was to deliver would already be dead. I can't imagine enduring labor while knowing full well that the other side of pain will only bring to birth death itself. It is simply unfathomable! Decades later, the tears still flowed as this dear couple grieved again. But they did so in hope. They hugged me, wept with me, and bore my pain, and we collectively grieved. They grieved for Melanie and me; I grieved for them. And in the midst of it, Easter broke into the tomb of my office. I looked at this faithful couple who had carried their grief unbeknownst to me, their pastor. But now, in the light of Easter morning, we were able—together—to hold tight to each other and to the promise of our God, who keeps us in life eternal. The Easter sermon for me that day was preached by this incredible couple who testified to a God who never let them go.

The Easter alleluias continued in the form of testimonies that the tellers now felt they had permission to share. One couple came to talk about their own D&C experience, and others talked about failed fertility treatments. A woman spoke frankly about her multiple miscarriages. Story after story was shared with me and with others in the community of saints gathered at my door. So, so many people had been wounded by their experience with fertility and pregnancy issues! Had I known at six o'clock that Easter morn the tidal wave of stories I was going to hear between worship services, I'm not sure I could have prepared for it. Likely, my grief would have compelled me to stay home; the thought of this torrent of pain might have been unbearable, given our experience and the fact that Melanie was recovering at home following our loss. Instead, the day became transformative for me. The stories, though grounded in the reality of death, spoke comfort and hope, trusting in the promise of life we celebrated on resurrection day.

I have come to believe that it was a Mary moment for the congregation. That is, by naming the truth of pregnancy loss, we became like Mary Magdalene in the garden, as told in John's Gospel. Fittingly, it is an Easter story. On the first Easter day, while weeping outside Jesus's empty tomb, Mary is approached by the resurrected Jesus, whom she does not recognize. He asks, "Woman, why are you weeping? Whom are you looking for?" (20:15). Mary has experienced the depths of death-induced grief, which has now been compounded by confusion and disorientation at the empty tomb. The verse continues as the narrative unfolds in this way: "Supposing him to be the gardener, she said to him, 'Sir, if you have carried him away, tell me where you have laid him, and will take him away.'" At that moment, Jesus utters one clear, life-altering word: "Mary."

In the wake of death, the God of life sees Mary and claims her as God's own. Mary's name on the lips of the resurrected Jesus pierces through her pain and discombobulation; it is a word of profound recognition and genuine solidarity. And ultimately, it is a word of healing and wholeness. God sees Mary and names her, and in turn, Mary knows she is seen and named by God. It is the power of resurrection at work! The Mary moment for our congregation on that Sunday was a time as community to name pregnancy loss in our prayers and, in doing so, to essentially name those in our midst who have suffered in this way. As a worshipping community, we stood together at the threshold of the empty tomb, many of us weeping at the sting of death. By the grace of God, our names hang on the lips of the one who conquers death and subsequently claims us in the healing dawn of resurrection life. In that Mary moment, I believe, many of us heard our pain named, and thus our identity as people wounded by reproductive issues was affirmed in public for the very first time.

Without question, I was shocked by the outpouring of people who spoke their truths of miscarriage, reproductive issues, and stillbirths because we were bold enough to name this concern aloud in worship. These issues are pervasive, but until that moment, I'd had no idea. Such suffering happens all too frequently, but who would know? In our society and in our church, we have failed to create safe space to share these truths. Since then, I have experienced profound testimonies by courageous women preaching and speaking in church on the hardships of pregnancy loss and fertility challenges—women like Ellie, Lauren, and Elizabeth, who spoke their truths, boldly naming their God who claimed them in their own grief and suffering. Their testimonies held in tension both death and resurrection, their own journeys through Maundy Thursday and Good Friday to Easter morning. I wept with them even as we professed our hope together in a God who does not abandon us unto death—our God in Christ Jesus, who, like Mary Magdalene, calls us by name and brings us from threshold of death into the light of life.

The church ought not be silent on issues of suffering and death. This is exactly where God meets us, and it is precisely where we need to be met. On that Easter morning following the loss of our baby, I still felt the pangs of Maundy Thursday. I give thanks to God for the community of the faithful—family, congregation members, friends—who sustained Melanie and me in those hours. I am grateful for that Easter morning and continue to experience that resurrection moment years later. For as I tap the recesses of my memory, I can still hear the resounding shouts of "Christ is risen!" that echoed from the sanctuary as the line of dear ones gathered at my office door. I will always remember how, with Easter all around us, we wept together at the suffering and loss that marks our bodies forever—that is, until the resurrected Christ has the final word for us all. In the meantime, we hold each other in loving faith, trusting that here and now, God is present. Is it enough? Thanks to the faith of others, I believe it is.

+ + +

At the outset of this book, I stated that these musings of mine reveal how my children have and continue to nourish my faith in God and fully manifest Christ's incarnate love in my life. I said that although I seek to parent in faith, I learn more about God from the children in my life than I could ever possibly hope to teach them. This chapter, though, speaks only of one child who was unborn and taken by anencephaly. Yet out of this near-unbearable sorrow, our unborn child taught me about the depth and breadth of God's love—a love that endures despite the bodily betrayal, the pervading sense of loss, and the shaken faith, and a love, through Christ Jesus, that holds tight to us through our suffering and death into healing and resurrection life. Our unborn fetus taught me more about faith than I can ever fully comprehend.

A few weeks after that Holy Week and the Maundy Thursday of Melanie's D&C, we took a brief vacation to Savannah, Georgia. My in-laws were visiting from Minnesota, and we wanted to see some of the historic sites. I remember sitting in the back of the van with Melanie as we drove away from a beach outside of Savannah. Her cell phone rang. On the other end was a lab technician. They had the definitive results of the genetic tests of the unborn fetus. Yes, it was anencephaly. Yes, the ten-week-old fetus, despite the healthy heart, never would have survived outside the womb. Yes, the cranium was not at all developed. And yes, the decision we had made was really no decision at all.

As she was receiving all the information from the medical professional, I watched Melanie's face, trying to read the conversation. Near the end of the phone call, I remember, she put her hand near her mouth with a slight intake of breath. She muttered a "thank you" into the phone and hung up. Tears welled up in her eyes. With a cracking voice, she said, "It was a boy." To this day, as I recall that moment in the back of the van, unbidden tears are summoned. Despite my best efforts, my body still betrays me. Like old friends, the tears find their way once again down my cheeks. The ground is all too familiar. The pain endures even amid all the joy we receive from our three healthy children, who gift us with love every moment of our lives. The death is real, even though we live in the hope of resurrection.

It was a boy. He was a boy. And he taught me so much about God.

5. Tooth Fairy

stewardship (noun): 1. wise and faithful use of God-given resources for the sake of serving the church and the world; 2. the ongoing challenge to see and act knowing that all that we are and all that we have are gifts from God; 3. the formation of a community learning together the truth of God's abundance in the face of a false—albeit dominant—narrative of scarcity; 4. a lifelong journey of giving of one's self, time, and possessions that seeks to follow the example of God's compassionate love in Christ Jesus.

Meet the Bink Fairy. If you haven't heard, she is the Tooth Fairy's younger sister. At times, the Bink Fairy goes by other names, such as the Nuk Fairy or the Paci Fairy, but in our house, she has always been called the Bink Fairy. Her name depends on what a family decides to call the nipple-mimicking soother cherished by countless babies and toddlers. Some people call them pacifiers ("paci" for short), and others use Nuk or some variation thereof, while folks in the United Kingdom often use *dummy* as the descriptor. Still others create their own unique titles for the suckling device. Our household went with the abridged version of *binky* and simply called it a bink. Thus, the Tooth Fairy's sibling was known by our family as the Bink Fairy. And the sole purpose of the Bink Fairy is, at the appointed time, to *steal* all the binks from the child, once and for all.

We, of course, did not create the Bink Fairy. The Bink Fairy has been hard at work for quite some time, flitting from house to house, swiping pacifiers from sleeping children. I really don't recall when or how we learned about her existence. Somehow the concept of the Bink Fairy found its way to us. Parents talk to parents, read parenting blogs or magazines, and seek advice from "experts" who have endured the trials of parenthood. In this case, the rigorous challenge of parenting is to permanently remove the sacred sucking tool from the clutches of a codependent child. Remember that many children have sucked on a bink since birth! That translates into day after day for hours on end and often throughout every night for months—years even. Taking away this prized possession is no easy task for a mere mortal; the delicate touch of a fairy may be required.

Of course, we create the problem to begin with by offering a bink to newborn babies. Each parent has to weigh the pros and cons of popping a silicone or rubber pacifier into their baby's mouth. The obvious pros include the ability to silence a crying or fussing baby. It is a near-magical moment to stick a soother in the quivering lips of a screaming child and watch her watery eyes blink themselves into a state of bliss. This immediate reaction doesn't happen every time, but often enough for parents to stash a bink in every room of the house and carry one on their person at all times. The ability to manufacture silence is a survival mechanism in the grocery store, on extended car rides, anywhere at 2:00 a.m., and of course, during worship. The bink can offer desperate parents moments of peace and respite in the relentless raucous reality of parenting babies. Hell, I've been tempted more than once to jam a bink into my six-year-old's mouth. Of course, I wouldn't *really* do it. Besides, the Bink Fairy had snatched them all away some time ago. That's probably best for everyone.

Eliminating the dependence on the bink is one of the major challenges of choosing the path of pacifier usage. Our two girls were both big fans of the bink; they loved to sleep with it in their mouths. So the bink did its job of soothing them to sleep, but a sleeping baby is prone to let the bink drop out of her mouth when in a deep REM cycle. The result? Sleep interrupted. All too often, we had to get out of bed several times during the night to simply place the bink back into their screaming mouths. The instant results were welcome, but the constant search in or around the crib for a discarded bink was tiresome. By the third or fourth nighttime stumble-walk to the girls' bedrooms, I might have cursed the bink aloud more than once. My cats might have heard a few four-letter words tumble out of my mouth in the hallway under the cover of night. But you would have to ask them; I plead the fifth.

Our son, however, did not take to the pacifier. In fact, he refused anything artificial, including bottles. I spent more than one tear-filled day trying to get Soren to drink breastmilk from a bottle. I mean, I really, truly, desperately, prayerfully tried to get him to take the bottle. Whatever the category beyond stubborn is, Soren makes his home there. This made life challenging for the whole household, but most of all for Melanie. Leaving work over your lunch hour to go breastfeed your baby is more than a pain in the ass (my words, not hers). There simply was no other way to feed our kid. Let me say it again: I tried to get that kid to take a bottle. I still have the emotional scars to prove it; perhaps Soren does, too.

Alas, Soren never took the bink. That made things a lot louder for us the third time around with a baby. Car rides were rough, as were many worship services. Deprived of the power to silently soothe, we had to leave the sanctuary space much more often during corporate worship than we ever had to with the girls. The child muzzle was no longer a viable tool in our parenting arsenal. What that meant, though, was simply this: no bink, no Bink Fairy. Soren's stubbornness meant his room was never graced by the Bink Fairy stealthily winging her way in the dark to claim her keep. Thus, Soren never received his prize from the Bink Fairy.

That's the thing: fairies can't just show up to take precious things and not leave something in their stead. The Tooth Fairy wouldn't be a popular fairy if she grabbed the teeth without making a deposit of one kind or another. Traditionally, the Tooth Fairy is known for leaving money under the pillows of sleeping gap-toothed children, whereas the Bink Fairy lugged in one big toy on her special night. Of course, because the Bink Fairy makes only one visit in a lifetime, her one gift needs to be special. The Tooth Fairy, however, is a repeat visitor, so cash seems to be the simpler, utilitarian choice. Whenever the Tooth Fairy comes to our house, she prefers to bring coins—specifically, quarters.

At the outset, we saw the visit from the Tooth Fairy as an opportunity to reinforce the teaching of stewardship in our home. If we were going to continue our foray into the world of make-believe alongside Santa Claus and the Easter Bunny, we were going to do so with an agenda. So along with the coins, the Tooth Fairy leaves instructional notes under our children's pillows. As it would happen, the Tooth Fairy is a poet. She's a bad poet, to be sure, but her earnest effort is commendable. When our first child lost her first tooth, the Tooth Fairy decided it was time to let loose her inner poet. She was inspired by wanting to make this first moment memorable, as well as her desire to cultivate gratitude in the heart of a young child. That night with Anya's first lost tooth under her pillow, the Tooth Fairy hastily though lovingly scribbled out her first poem. Actually, she typed it on a Mac computer. She's a twenty-first-century fairy, apparently, with access to computers, printers, and mobile devices. I suspect a handwritten note might have raised a few questions, as her handwriting may look suspiciously like mine. So on eight-and-a-half-by-eleven-inch paper in Bradley Hand font with three silver quarters taped to the page, the winged amateur poet placed this piece under Anya's pillow:

> You lost your first tooth, and I am so proud.
> I flew into your room. Shhh! Not so loud.
> Asleep in your bed, you sure did not hear.

Under your pillow three quarters appeared.
One quarter to spend however you wish,
Another quarter to save and cherish.
Finally, one quarter: please give it away,
And share it with others, for this I pray!

I'll be honest, I was proud of this parenting moment. The poetry was sloppy, but I was employing the legend of the Tooth Fairy to teach the importance of giving unto others. Yet as I stood there with some parental pride, listening to Anya read the note aloud, I was not at all ready for her reaction when she came to the end: she wept. The poem was poorly written, certainly, but I didn't think it was awful enough to bring tears to a six-year-old. But it wasn't the poetry that spurred on the tears; it was the Tooth Fairy's request for my daughter to give something away. In the shadow of the wings of the Tooth Fairy, we learned together that the prospect of giving unto others can be painful exercise. I am happy to say, however, that this story does not end with Anya's tears.

+ + +

Years ago, I began a call as a solo pastor in Minneapolis at the outset of stewardship season. In other words, the first four sermons I preached to my new congregation were about money. They were about other things as well, but the thrust of the average stewardship season is to ask members to commit financially to the mission of the church for the year ahead. In light of Anya's personal revelation from the Tooth Fairy's poem, I can safely say that giving can be painful. As difficult as giving can be, it pales in comparison to speaking publicly about money. And not just speaking about money, but asking for it as well. Requesting money for four Sundays from a group of near-strangers is its own exploration of one's pain threshold, for the preacher and congregation members alike.

Prior to my arrival, one member of the congregation serving on the church council had proposed that the church's stewardship campaign be modeled after Joash's chest, and the idea was accepted. When I was told this information my first day or two as their pastor, I nodded and smiled politely. But inside, my mind was racing: "Who the hell is Joash, and what does his chest have to do with stewardship?" It helps to know that "chest" doesn't refer to Joash's torso, but rather a chest or trunk to store important items, including money. Helpful indeed! It turns out that the Bible is very a big book, and this pastor doesn't remember every Bible story. My ignorance regarding Joash and his chest sent me back to my office library to dust off some of my books.

In my study, I discovered that in his brief cameo in the Bible (in 2 Kings and 2 Chronicles), Joash reigned as the ninth king of Judah for nearly forty years. Scholars disagree on the exact years of his rule, but they agree that his years bookend 800 BCE. In his time, Joash decided to "restore the house of the Lord"—namely, to repair and care for the temple in Jerusalem. To do so, he instructed the Levites (priests) to collect taxes for the restoration project. Here's how it relates to Joash's chest:

> So the king [Joash] gave command, and they [Levites] made a chest, and set it outside the gate of the house of the Lord. A proclamation was made throughout Judah and Jerusalem to bring in for the Lord the tax that Moses the servant of God laid on Israel in the wilderness. All the leaders and all the people rejoiced and brought their tax and dropped it into the chest until it was full. Whenever the chest was brought to the king's officers by the Levites, when they saw that there was a large amount of money in it, the king's secretary and the officer of the

chief priest would come and empty the chest and take it and return it to its place. So they did day after day, and collected money in abundance. (2 Chronicles 24:8–14)

I know my eyes passed over this story when required to read the whole Bible as part of my seminary studies, but honestly, it was not memorable. (Your eyes have probably glossed over it just now, too, but bear with me, there is a point!) Though the story was for me forgettable, I was now given the task of using it for a stewardship sermon series and thus acutely if not forcibly interested.

This is an example of proof-texting—namely, plucking a biblical passage out of its context and using it interpretively for your own end goals. Around stewardship season, we church leaders search for stories that seek to stir people toward faithful giving, and I fully admit my guilt in proof-texting Joash and his chest for the sake of meeting the missional budget of the church. Somewhat comically, we at the church took our cue from Joash and put out an antique little chest in the front of the sanctuary. Seriously, the chest looked like it came from Joash's storage closet, if not the hull of a pirate ship. There the two-foot-by-one-foot chest sat on a pedestal for four Sundays as I preached on stewardship to God's mission; the gifts of time, talent, and money from God used to serve God; and the abundance in our midst. And like Joash, "day after day," we "collected money in abundance." Okay, not exactly. But congregation members did come forward at the end of the four Sundays and placed pledge cards for the year's giving in the chest. That was powerful to watch; I think we fell short of our goal by only about $5,000 or $6,000. In my world, that's a victory! Thanks, Joash, to you and your chest.

In recent days, I thought of Joash and his chest in an altogether different context. It was time in the Lind-Ayres household to clean out the basement. Our downstairs always looks as if toys are incessantly breeding. The influx of Christmas and birth-day gifts from family and friends create tidal waves of toys that threaten to sweep our children away. All of them were given with loving intent, but our toys surpass the threshold needed in any one house. It is a constant lesson of materialism's insidious hold on our lives. To combat this issue and to create space, we periodi-cally purge the toys by sharing with others. We put out a bin and start collecting items we will donate to children who don't have any or as many toys. All three kids participate in this exercise as they reluctantly comb through their own stuff and decide what stays and what goes. And I wait, like Joash, for the bin to collect toys in abundance. It's one long-ass wait.

Understandably, this is a challenging exercise for anyone, let alone young children. We all know that our possessions tend to own us, and letting go can be excruciating. How, as parents, do we teach our kids to let go when we have such a tough time ourselves? In Matthew 19, Jesus encounters a young rich man intent on inheriting eternal life. Jesus says to him, "If you wish to be perfect, go, sell your possessions, and give the money to the poor, and you will have treasure in heaven; then come, follow me." The man's reaction ought not surprise us: "When the young man heard this word, he went away grieving, for he had many possessions." I am certain that all have felt the grief of letting go of our possessions. And our toy-bin collection in the spirit of Joash's chest educed much consternation and eventually grief with Anya, Svea, and Soren.

What I thought was about an hour-long project to clean out and organize the basement turned into a frustrating weeklong process. The kids put next to nothing in the bin. We examined every truck, doll, block, stuffed animal, board game, and book under the roof. Yes or no? Gift unto others or keep for ourselves? The vote by the trio to give away the item was typically "no." To their credit, they each slipped a few smaller items into the bin, saying things like "Another kid can have this" or "Here, Dad, let's give this away." But looking at the accumulated mass of toys overflowing in our basement, the few items dropped into the bin were like droplets of water extracted from a full bathtub.

So I took matters into my own hands. Without their permission, I began throwing into the bin items that I knew they rarely touched. Every time I did so, the kids would protest. Suddenly some party favor trinket from a long-forgotten birthday party became a child's dearest treasure. And with my back turned, the abundance I had placed in Joash's toy bin would mysteriously vanish. It was an exercise in futility. Each time I argued with them that they never played with the toy and some other child would truly enjoy it, they countered with just how special the toy was to them. Occasionally, they would offer another toy in its stead, a weak display of self-sacrifice, as their offering was often a busted toy destined for the trash, not another child's home. Letting go is hard work. I persisted, for this was a teachable moment for my kids—and for me.

In this painful process, I discovered that I had a few untouchable toys as well. Svea's Little People horse stable was one of them. After all, this was the special gift that had arrived airmail via the Bink Fairy. It was now four years old and rarely touched by anyone except friends who came to visit. (Another kid's—or adult's—toys are often more appealing than one's own.) But when I picked it up for consideration for the bin, I suddenly saw Svea's bink-sucking baby face staring at me. A flood of emotions stirred within me as this toy—this thing—represented time that had swiftly passed us by. Parents of older children and especially grandparents often tell new parents to enjoy the time with little ones because it is gone before you know it. As I clutched the Bink Fairy's gift in my hand, I realized it was proof of the cliché's truth. I now held an artifact of Svea's babyhood that was forever gone.

In that moment, I entered deep into the pain of my children. Letting go is so hard, and I was not ready to let this toy go. Another time, perhaps, but not then. I suppose I hoped to cling, if for a few moments, to the time when the Bink Fairy had created mystique for my kids. Her days were over, and her special gifts were no longer the treasures they once had been. Instead, they were eating up space in our basement and needed to find a new home and a child to love them. But I couldn't do it. Like the rich man in Matthew, I grieved at the thought of letting this go. My heart ached while I held the Bink Fairy's gift of a large plastic pastel horse stable. I certainly was mindful of my tears as I discreetly wiped them away, trying to fill the bin with things other than the horse stable. To this day, the horse stable is still in our basement. I'm still not at a point to let it go. I will some-day—when I'm ready.

The bin remained pitifully low as the hour-long project extended out for several days. We periodically pushed the kids to add more treasures to Joash's toy chest, but our efforts were met with minimal success as more toys were "saved" from the bin by clingy children. I decided to expedite the now-lagging project by filling the chest to overflowing abundance when the kids were sleeping. The lesson on stewardship for the children would have to be suspended in this moment and resumed another time; I needed to get the basement purged and organized and move on with life. The night before the trip to the donation site, I added several toys that were, from my perspective, neglected and underutilized. They would not be missed, or so I thought.

Weeks later, Anya and Svea were playing together in the base-ment as they had done several times following our painful stew-ardship exercise. When I went to check on them, they were deep in imaginative play with small plastic princesses sold by a particular company that also specializes in talking mice and roller coasters. It is a beautiful and all-too-often fleeting moment when my kids are playing together without any drama or nonsense. So I took a moment to watch as the girls were sprawled out on the floor, surrounded by a horde of their miniaturized royal characters. Then came the question from Svea: "Dad, where is the pink princess castle? We can't find it." Shit!

Both girls looked up from the floor at me, and I hesitated to respond. One look at my panicked face, and they knew. It was uncanny. Svea immediately bellowed an agonized cry, "You gave it away!" She began to wail. The princess castle had been Anya's, gifted to her by Santa Claus when she was two. Six years seemed long enough because it had been lying dormant in our cluttered basement. My face must have confirmed Svea's accusation, for Anya's eyes welled up in response. I had brought both girls to tears by what I had thought was a judicious decision. My nomination for World's Greatest Dad would have to wait yet again. I felt like crap. This lesson in giving made me look and feel like a ruthless, if not heartless, parent. Despite my efforts to comfort my emotionally wounded daughters, they continued to cry while spurning my attempts to hug and hold them. When the howling and sobbing finally ceased, I received the silent treatment for much of the afternoon. From my daughters' perspective, silence was just punishment administered in accordance to my grievous action. Giving is painful to learn and equally painful to teach.

+ + +

The Bible speaks about just and responsible use of our resources for the uplifting of our neighbors more than nearly any other topic. In fact, the Bible has more to say about faithfully guiding God's people in compassionate stewardship than it has to say about sex or salvation. The Bible frequently and consistently addresses the temptation and harm of materialism. Not mincing words, 1 Timothy 6:9–11 is but one example: "Those who want to be rich fall into temptation and are trapped by senseless and harmful desires that plunge people into ruin and destruction. For the love of money is the root of all kinds of evil, and in their eagerness to be rich some have wandered away from the faith and pierced themselves with many pains. But as for you, people of God, shun all this; pursue righteousness, godliness, faith, love, endurance, gentleness." In our consumer-obsessed society, however, sex and salvation tend to garner more attention from the media, rather than the soul-sucking power of overconsumption and the hording of resources. I'm not pointing a finger; I think Christians of every stripe tend to get quiet when it comes to leaning into our faith and condemning our harmful practices relating to wealth. I certainly need to do better, and I recognize the task can feel very daunting, given our cultural context and the pervasive power of materialism in our lives.

Melanie and I battle consumerist impulses daily and seek to stave off the duplicitous narrative espoused by our culture. It's not easy. Nevertheless, we try to be faithful stewards and give financially to our church and other nonprofits that have earned our allegiance by their work for the sake of others. This, too, is not easy. The torrent of living expenses, our outstanding school loan payments, and our desire to save for our children's education all pull at our bank account, leaving us to feel as if we have little to give.

Early in our marriage, however, we would start our budget planning by asking each other, "How much will we give away this year?" Instead of waiting to see what was left over to give away, we gave out of the abundance of what we had received. The church gave us verbiage for this approach, calling it "first fruits" giving. I think it is one way to flip the narrative, as the gospel of Jesus is wont to do. We seek to act in response to our belief in the abundant gifts and grace of God. Thus, we are called to steward those gifts in ways that serve others in the name of grace. Admittedly, our family is still growing into this way of being. We have failed often, yet the journey of faith compels us to ask again and again, "How can we give more of ourselves in the name of Jesus?" The task can be overwhelming, and conversations hard.

So I recommend starting simple; let us start with the children in our midst. For even the Tooth Fairy can be an entry point into having faithful conversations about the beliefs and practices that we as a family apply in living out our call to share the gospel of Jesus. Something as silly as a winged magical creature can become an avenue for engaging parents and children together in the call and challenge to share God's gifts with the world. I'm not necessarily suggesting that the Tooth Fairy become a mascot for the Christian faith and our approach to money (though it isn't my worst idea, given the fairy's attention to good stewardship in tandem with her mystical power of flight and remarkable omniscience with regard to dental health). She makes for a compelling tool to teach stewardship, as my children tend to listen more to a fairy than to their father.

In our home, the Tooth Fairy's first foray into poetry set the stage for the general theme and thrust of each bad poem to follow. A literary analysis of her first work reveals three themes relating to the use of material wealth: spend, save, and share. The Tooth Fairy gave Anya permission to spend a portion of her gift on herself, something we all enjoy doing from time to time. But we need to temper spending habits with healthy saving practices. This was fun for Anya, too, as she joyfully placed one quarter into her Winnie the Pooh piggy bank. It was the third part about giving and sharing that brought her to tears.

I suppose one can rightfully ask, "What does my tooth have to do with other people?" That is, how does the pain of pulling out my own tooth that I grew and cared for in my own mouth for some six years become the business of someone else? A robust theology of stewardship begins with an assumption that all we are and all we have—even our baby teeth—are, in fact, God's. This approach to stewardship gives theological legs to our household's Tooth Fairy experiment with our children while naming the practical realities of the stewardship journey. How do we practice stewardship together as a family and weave it into the fabric of our daily routine? Or how do we continue to grow as parents in faith who are seeking to teach the truth of God's abundance to our kids despite the deceptive contrary narrative at work in the world? How might we make room for God's compassionate love to inspire the complexities of daily living in ways that open our hearts to the challenge and joy of giving? For me, reframing the Tooth Fairy's teachings beyond the important practicalities of spending, saving, and sharing toward a deeper practice of stewardship has been a surprising gift to me and, I hope, a gift to my children.

Anya's immediate response to the Tooth Fairy's poem was to cry. That was an unsettling surprise to me. For starters, bringing my child to tears when a particular experience is supposed to be joyful makes me feel like an ass. I had thought I was marking the moment with a fun message from a fairy; instead, I shat all over the moment, inserting a complicating situation for my daughter. Yet if you are a six-year-old and a fairy gives you a task, no matter the anguish, you do it. And that's what Anya did.

Once the shock wore off and the tears ended, we talked with her about the importance of sharing with others. Despite her red face and drippy nose from her crying spell, Anya was able to nod her agreement to heed the Tooth Fairy's request. Harnessing her capacity to see beyond the immediate moment, Anya looked at us and declared, "I want to give my quarter to church." Now I was surprised in an altogether new way. Once she had shaken off the pain, Anya was able to quickly determine where her gift ought to go. And of course, my heart was warmed by her choice. All we have begins with and belongs to God, and her selection reinforced for me that she was beginning to grasp the practice of this theology lived out in the weekly rhythm of worshipping life together.

The Sunday following her tooth loss and complex reaction to the Tooth Fairy's poem, Anya remembered on her own to bring her quarter to church. She, like her mother, takes her commitments very seriously. When the offering plate was passed that day, I was inspired by her capacity to give. The quarter dropped into the golden plate, and Anya's face beamed with a deep sense of accomplishment. She had fulfilled the request of the Tooth Fairy, but more than that, she had given from her heart to the work and witness of the church. The pain of giving had given way to the compassionate act of sharing God's abundance with others. Had this enterprise lacked Anya's expression of anguish at the command to give, I really don't think I would have learned as much about the call to steward God's gifts. That is, if she had complied with the Tooth Fairy without tearful resistance, my experience wouldn't have yielded my own deep reflection. The painful journey to drop her quarter into the offering plate made the gift a much more powerful witness; a simple quarter became a gift of love that continues to inspire me to this day.

Apparently, the Tooth Fairy also was inspired, for her bad poetry kept coming. Anya's second tooth yielded a near replica of the first poem with the exact call to share, save, and spend a portion of her earnings. The rhyming scheme and vocabulary were different, but it was essentially the same message. The result? Tearless joy! The expectations were now set, and the coins accompanied by the notes were now the norm. Without thinking twice, Anya set aside the portion to be given to the church. The church was now her default mission to share her gifts with others; I did not object. More coins populated our church's offering plate the next Sunday.

With the expectations established, the Tooth Fairy did not need to be as explicit about how much money Anya needed to give. On January 22, 2016, Anya lost her third tooth. I remember the date because it was Anya's seventh birthday, as noted by the Tooth Fairy's poem:

> On your birthday, dear Anya, I had a hunch
> That you would lose your third tooth while eating lunch!
> And sure enough, that top one finally came out.
> With a wink and my wand, I fluttered about,
> To your home and pillow, to bring you, my dear,
> Seven quarters this time, one coin for each year.
> You now know what to do, so be kind and be smart.
> Share your gifts with others and give from your heart!

With seven quarters in hand, "one coin for each year," Anya set aside two to give to our church. Again, a simple act yielded growth in her understanding of stewardship. She received more from the fairy, so she gave more to the mission of the church. She initiated and executed that decision on her own—again, a moment of pride for her dad. Like most things, giving gets easier the more you do it.

The Tooth Fairy's foray into poetry has been a commitment all its own. My whimsical decision to honor Anya's first lost tooth has now become an ongoing undertaking in the spirit of fairness. I didn't make this realization until about the fourth poem or so. As I was tinkering with a poem, Melanie said, "You know, Anya has a lot of teeth. And so do the other kids. Are you going to do this for every tooth?" The truth was, I hadn't thought about it. Three mouths with some twenty baby teeth would require sixty poems. That's a lot of roughshod poems written hastily in the dark of the night! The Lind-Ayres children have come to expect the Tooth Fairy's crafted notes along with their gift of cold, hard cash. So like it or not, I'm committed. The joy that comes from every bad poem written under the pressure of impending dawn is that each note creates an opportunity to live out stewardship for our household.

And then there is that time when a child initiates communication with the Tooth Fairy. A few months ago, Anya had a loose tooth that was bothering her. It was a stubborn bugger and would not come out, despite wiggling and whatnot. Anya took matters into her own hands—as she often does—and wrote a note to the Tooth Fairy, seeking her advice. She wanted to know how to get her tooth out. A fair question. Her note of inquiry was folded up and placed under her pillow. Makes perfect sense! How else do you communicate with the Tooth Fairy but through your pillow-turned-mailbox? When your child writes a note to the Tooth Fairy, a response is required. My task of writing sixty poems had gotten bigger. With this added assignment, I decided to take the message of financial stewardship and expand it to stewardship of body. So here's what I wrote:

> Anya, my dear, your question is good.
> What should you do? Well, I have hunch.
> The answer you seek has to do with food:
> More vegetables, more fruit, more things that go crunch.
> For if you eat more of these, your teeth will come out.
> Of this I am certain; I have no doubt.
> With love and a bright smile,
> The Tooth Fairy

How do you get your kids to eat healthier as a way to steward God's gift of our bodies? That's a mystery we are still seeking to solve in our household. But enlisting help from the Tooth Fairy to encourage kids to eat more fruits and vegetables can't hurt. On another note, I noticed that the Tooth Fairy often repeats words like *out* and *hunch* and *dear*. The fairy may need a creative-writing class to expand her rhyming vocabulary!

Anya's experience with the Tooth Fairy has (re)taught the whole family to, in her poetic instruction, "give from the heart." By following the directions of the fairy, Anya has modeled for her younger siblings the way to give. With a watchful eye on her older sister, Svea quickly became accustomed to giving away a portion of her earnings. In one note, the Tooth Fairy had asked Svea to "do your loving part" and give two out of her six quarters to others. Beaming with a new gap-toothed grin, Svea packed her quarters into her pocket on a Sunday morning as our church once again became the recipient of hard-earned quarters. Giving is learned behavior, and children are probably some of our best teachers! For our part, Melanie and I, in full cooperation and partnership with the Tooth Fairy, continue to cultivate compassionate hearts in our household, learning the pattern and developing the propensity for the faithful stewardship of God's gifts.

+ + +

Melanie and I have—imperfectly—committed to model and teach stewardship to our children. We continue to hope and pray that we can bear witness as a household to the wondrous love of God outpoured in the gift of Christ Jesus. We seek to gift our kids with a grounded perspective through the theology of abundance that breaks our world's persuasive albeit false narrative of scarcity. When I actually trust God enough to believe in the truth of divine abundance, my own consumerist-individualistic-materialistic heart, shaped by a North American culture, shatters. The shards of my heart are pieced back together by our God, who is able to make all things new. I have discovered that my children are often the people God uses to pick up these shards of my shattered heart. Like little surgeons, my kids get to work reconstructing my heart through their own witness to God's call. Children have the power to fix our hearts like no other!

When Anya was enthusiastically preparing for her sixth birthday party, Melanie and I had a revelation. Likely, Melanie was the sole proprietor of the revelation, but my shoddy memory enables me to believe I had something to do with it. The revelation was this: no gifts! Our basement was already teeming with toys from the fallout of Christmas. Consumerism had avalanched the birth of Jesus yet again. It was January, and we were in desperate need of a toy purge; we needed another Joash's chest. The thought of another landslide of toys spilling into the basement was unwelcome. So no gifts—that is, no gifts for Anya.

Along with the birthday announcements, we explicitly stated, "We kindly request no gifts for Anya. Instead, you are invited to bring nonperishable food items that will be donated to our local food shelf." The gifts in honor of Anya's sixth birthday were food items for people struggling with food insecurity. We made this decision as part of our ongoing journey with our kids regarding stewardship and our call to serve others. It was a teachable moment, to be sure, and I was so proud of how Anya handled it.

When we sat her down to discuss the reality that she would not be getting gifts at her birthday party, she was sad. There were no tears, but she was very disappointed, which, I think, is justifiable for a near-six-year-old dreaming about her birthday party. We assured her that she would receive a few presents from family members, including her parents. But the party would be a time to celebrate with friends, play games, eat homemade pizza, and share what we have with others. We told her that people would be encouraged to bring food items, which we would take to church to be donated to the local food shelf. She understood and was supportive of the idea. I think the promise of presents from other folks helped pave the way to understanding.

I see Melanie's revelatory insight as a gift to all involved. First, it was a gift to the ten families sending a child over to our house for Anya's party. Those families didn't have to travel to a store or log in to Amazon to purchase something they had no idea if Anya already owned or would even want. We parents do that enough with the tidal wave of birthday parties that hit in elementary school. Second, it was a gift for Melanie and me. We did not have to deal with another influx of stuff in a house that already has more than enough. Third, it was a gift to Anya and by extension our other two kids. They learned in a new way how to think about and give to others, even on a day that is set up to be entirely self-focused. And finally, it was a gift to the people who would ultimately receive the food items.

On the day of Anya's party, the response was incredible. Our "gift table," which had previously been reserved for presents for the birthday girl, was overflowing with nonperishable food items. I distinctly remember another parent, while dropping her twin daughters off for the party, holding a bag full of food and asking, "How did you do this? There would be a riot in our household!" My answer came with a shrug: "I don't know. We just did it." It wasn't magic. We just made a decision to do it, thus weaving into our family's birthday rituals an attention to our responsibility and call to share God's abundance with others. It has been life-giving for us!

Now we let the kids pick where they want gifts to go. For instance, upon Svea's sixth birthday party (the kids' age we begin this custom), she had a kitty-themed birthday—not a surprising choice for our little animal lover. But Svea also decided, in tandem with her theme and passion for animals, that she wanted people to bring money for the Humane Society of the United States. Her birthday invitations asked people to give online or bring a donation to the party—but no gifts for Svea. Incredibly, Svea was as excited about the donations as anything else for her party, save the cupcakes.

Just this past year, I was at a school play for Anya. The twin girls who have been Anya's classmates in elementary school and frequented Anya's birthday parties in years past shared the makeshift stage with Anya and all the others in her grade. There I bumped into the twins' mother, the same parent who had been shocked at our substituting nonperishable food items for Anya's presents two years before. When she saw me, she exclaimed, "Thank you! We did no gifts this year for the girls. Instead, we collected money for charity. It was wonderful! Thank you for the idea." Her girls didn't riot after all! Giving, though a challenge at times, also rewards the giver. I am so grateful for our children's ability to grow in their way of giving, as they have become models for their friends. Giving is contagious; consequently, kids are probably the best way to spread it.

From the Tooth Fairy to birthday-party gifts, we strive to embrace and embody stewardship as a household. Together as family, we are committed to muddling through the complexity of living into God's counternarrative of abundant love. It is a lifelong endeavor; we fail often. But the Christian pilgrimage is that—a pilgrimage. Together we journey each day, striving to live into the truth of God's abundance in our lives and sharing that abundance with others. My children have been the greatest companions on this journey, teaching my heart how to give anew and inspiring me to be a better steward of all of God's gifts.

In the spirit of gratitude and giving, I offer this brief word to the Tooth Fairy:

Thank you! Thank you for teaching our family about stewardship. I don't even mind the bad poetry. And if you see your younger sister, the Bink Fairy, please tell her that I miss her dearly.

6. Graveside

funeral (noun): 1. since the memory of humanity, the ritual moment marking the death of a person; 2. in the Christian tradition, the worship service and burial of a person where the dead body is physically present; 3. a taboo word in contemporary American culture, often avoided for actually daring to address death; 4. the heartbreaking yet beautiful moment in the pilgrimage of a believer in Christ Jesus when they travel, accompanied by loved ones, from death to resurrection-life.

Graveside, I held my daughter Svea's hand. She had just turned four that summer. Together we watched as my grandfather's casket was awkwardly lowered into the ground. It was real and tender and holy. I worried about Svea, though, as she watched the family weep and utter our teary goodbyes. The parent in me wanted to protect her from the sting of death; nevertheless, I knew in my grieving heart that there was no other place in the world she—we—could be at that moment. Together, we needed to walk this journey with the whole family. I trusted that out of our experience at the grave, Svea would encounter the sure and certain hope of the resurrection proclaimed in our gathering. In faith, I held her hand in mine and silently prayed as the casket descended into the earth.

My mother, Vivian, is the oldest of ten children born to Minnesota farmers and raised in the country. Married in their teens, her parents—my grandparents Melvin and Ellen—farmed fertile land near Appleton, Minnesota, the whole of their lives. Children of German and Norwegian immigrants, they had a work ethic that enabled them to survive near-poverty while raising enough children to fill a basketball court with A and B squads. My mother was twenty-one when her youngest sibling was born, so their three-bedroom farmhouse endured hordes of kids home at any given time but never all at once. Still, when I walk through the updated and modernized farmhouse these days, I swear I can hear the beleaguered floorboards moaning in agony from the incessant usage they received.

It was a glorious experience to grow up with our large family. When I was a kid, every visit to Grandpa and Grandma's farm meant a gaggle of cousins to chase around the acreage. Cornfields, hay bales, and wide-open spaces became our playground, while tractors (immobile), horses, chickens, and barnyard kittens became our playthings. On Thanksgiving Day, we had enough family members for legitimate teams to play tackle football in the snow, while Fourth of July gatherings had us playing baseball in the open field. There was never a shortage of bodies for games and mischief.

My parents raised my older brother, Shane; my younger sister, Krista; and me in faith with family at our center. They taught us the importance of family prioritizing family gatherings, and they taught us the importance of God's love for us by prioritizing church together. When my mother worked her hospital night shifts as a nurse, my father, James (Jim), took the three of us to worship and Sunday school on his own. That deep commitment on their part has made me the faithful parent (and pastor!) that I am today. Never—even in my stubborn and self-centered teen years—did I question my parents' love for me and my siblings, their love for our large extended family, or their love for God. They weren't perfect parents, but they were the best I could have asked for. I am still learning from them and am ever grateful they are such involved grandparents in the lives of all their grandchildren, whom they adore. I'm not surprised, given how family was central to the core of our life together. And on my mother's side, there was a lot of family to go around!

Because of the age span of the ten children birthed by

Grandma Ellen, I now have cousins the same age as my children. It's wild. In August 2015, I had to do the math: ten children, thirty-four grandchildren, and thirty-five great-grandchildren. The numbers have changed since then in both celebration and sadness. But at that moment in time, our immediate family unit had eighty-one persons, including Grandpa and Grandma. Our annual family fish fry in Appleton in early August was enough, I think, to cause an economic boon for a small town that hovers around a thousand people. The gas station, hotel, grocery store, and bar of choice (because even small Minnesota towns usually have more than one bar) no doubt felt the impact of our event. But in 2015, Appleton in August was overrun by our family on two occasions: the fish fry on August 8 and my grandfather's funeral on August 25.

Grandpa Melvin had suffered from kidney failure for some years, and in the end, the shadow of cancer was cast over him as well. Sadly, too many of us are acquainted with cancer, as it looms large in our world. If I could, I would spit in the direction of cancer, just as the early Christians would spit facing the west, the place where the sun sets as the darkness swallows the light. Given the ubiquity of cancer, it is impossible to pick any one direction to spit, so I'll just swallow my spit for now.

Melvin died at home (in town, as the family farm had been acquired by Uncle Mike and his family), days after the necessary decision to cease dialysis treatment for his failing kidneys. In Grandpa's last days, the door was constantly revolving, as children, grandchildren, and great-grandchildren came from near and far to say tear-choked goodbyes. A handful of family members, including my mother (a retired dialysis nurse, amazingly enough), kept constant vigil with my Grandma Ellen. Though painful for him and us, Grandpa's final hours were also filled with holy moments held in love and carried by grace of God.

I know Grandpa's pastor came to provide comfort and Holy

Communion. I know his children offered Bible readings and prayers together, including the shared words of the Lord's Prayer, which hovered on the lips of our dear dying Melvin. I know his grandchildren offered words of love and leave-taking. I know great-grandchildren, unable to fully grasp the gravity of his dying, shared wordless gestures of this same love through hugs and kisses. For my part, I drove the three hours from the urban hub of the Twin Cities to rural Greater Minnesota when Grandpa was spending much of his time restlessly resting. I went to see Grandpa but also to share time with Grandma and my mom.

I made the trek alone as an ambassador for Melanie and the kids. The five of us had knowingly said our goodbyes to Grandpa at the fish fry earlier that month. As a parent, you have to strategize when young children and travel are involved. We knew a trip was coming with the funeral. Throughout our parenting years, we have heard various opinions on how—if at all—you involve kids in death and dying. Melanie and I consider it essential to our life together as family in all its fullness. Preparing for Melvin's imminent death with our goodbyes already said, we confidently rested in our earlier words and actions. But despite my mother's assurances otherwise, I sensed my trip was needed. And it was—mostly for me. Death and dying are tricky times to negotiate with family and friends, but I say, When in doubt, show up! Presence is everything.

I showed up for a few hours that day, and it became the most profound experience I ever had with my grandpa. Upon my arrival, Grandpa was sleeping. I knew that actual rest was essential, given his sleepless nights of discomfort. I quickly reconciled with the fact that my trip might not result in a face-to-face visit with him. As a pastor, I certainly have had those kinds of moments in hospital rooms and visits to people on their deathbeds. Had that been true, my time with my grandma, mother, and aunt would have been healing enough. This I know. But two hours into the visit, Melvin stirred. My mother and Grandma Ellen went into his room, and minutes later, they accompanied him with his walker out to the kitchen table, where we were visiting.

When he saw me, it took him a moment before recognition was reflected back to me in his eyes. And then he smiled—truly smiled with his whole being. His bodily demeanor changed in a flash, and that look, that posture, that face, that smile form the memory my mind usually conjures first when I think of my grandpa. I believe with all my heart that if I ever see the face of Christ, it will look a whole hell of a lot like that!

And here's the thing: my grandpa was not an effusive man. Far from it. In fact, three words I would use to describe him are stoic, stubborn, and staid. He was an archetype of a German, Midwestern farmer born on the eve of the Great Depression. His farm-calloused hands were emblematic of his hard exterior surface. I never saw him cry, and only late in life did I personally hear the words *I love you* on his lips. That's not to say he didn't fiercely love us or have deep passion for his wife, his kids, their offspring, and their offspring's offspring. He did. But his love was like the farmland; the rich soil was hidden below a rocky surface. It was always there, but buried deep. The day I last spoke with my grandfather was probably the only time I saw the riches of his heart fully and unabashedly exposed. And what a sight!

After my grandfather settled himself into a seat at the kitchen table, we spoke for a little while about his childhood. He was hard of hearing—the toll of nearly eight decades of loud farm equipment sputtering in his ear. So I spoke strategically, asking him to talk about the Lutheran church and schoolhouse located just a few miles from the family farm. They had been instrumental in his life and the life of our family. It was refreshing to hear and see how he held the place of his faith near his heart. I wonder why we too often wait until the end to allow ourselves to be authentically open to one another. I know that this is not always true, and sometimes these moments are missed altogether or even are the occasion for greater pain and discord. I suppose the sacredness of dying is, at its core, an exercise of vulnerability. This may be one of death's blessings or curses for us—a blessing if we embrace the vulnerability and a curse if we repel it. And let's be honest: vulnerability often scares us all the way to death.

Then it happened. Melvin, my non-effusive grandfather, looked at me and asked, "Could you speak at my funeral?" What?! If my mother, aunt, and grandmother hadn't been in the room with me, I would have shouted for someone to come and witness his request. My grandfather, who had never asked anything of me in my entire life, just asked if I would speak at his funeral! I was dumbstruck. My jaw hit the kitchen table. Tears welled up in my eyes. What he was asking, really, was for his grandson-pastor to preach at his funeral. There is nowhere to hide in moments of holy wonder. They come, unprompted, and all you can do is embrace them with a heart bursting with gratitude. After collecting myself, I muttered, "Of course. It would be my honor." And I took his hand, a touch to accompany the promise.

At that point, I don't remember exactly what happened. The shock of his request was still reverberating throughout my body. I think a prayer was said, and Grandpa asked to return to his bed. He had, I believe, accomplished the task that was on his heart at the moment, and his body began to grow heavy again. I said my final goodbye in awe of a God who gifted me with this man, this family, this moment. Imperfect though we may be—and trust me, my family is very imperfect—moments of perfection sneak up on us and steal our breath away.

Some fifty-four hours following that table conversation, Melvin

Adolph Munsterman, child of God, died. Into your hands, O Merciful God, we entrust Melvin, a sheep of your own flock, a sinner of your own redeeming.

+ + +

When we sat Anya, Svea, and Soren down (as much as a one-year-old can sit down!) to tell them that Grandpa Melvin had died, they knew in their own way that it had been coming. They had hugged him goodbye at the family fish fry a week prior with our explanation that it would likely be the last time they saw him. Also, before and after my final visit with Melvin, I had told the kids that he was dying. Each time became an opportunity to explain death in ways I hoped they might understand. It's not an easy task, given that we adults don't fully understand death. We understand death biologically, to be sure, but spiritually, death is rife with mystery. And explaining mystery to little developing concrete-sequential thinkers is a challenge.

We gathered the kids on one of girls' beds. Since it was morning, it seemed like as good of a place as any and gave us more of an excuse to snuggle close together in this tender moment. We spoke to them slowly, intentionally. "Kids, Great-Grandpa Melvin died last night." There was a long, pregnant pause. I had already shed tears during my car ride home two days earlier, in my private prayers, and more recently, earlier that morning, on the phone when my mother shared the news with us. Now my focus was on the kids and their grief with Melvin's death. Svea broke the silence: "Is he with Jesus?" We responded, "Yes, Great-Grandpa Melvin is with Jesus."

Svea's question served as a testament to our parenting in faith. We taught our children about death and resurrection life in Christ Jesus, and it was a message our Christian community proclaimed in our worship often. I found reassurance in knowing that Svea associated death with the care of Jesus. I must admit, however, I sometimes think the quick "he's with Jesus" or "now he's in heaven" response is too simplistic. I'm not entirely sure why I think that, given that Jesus himself gave such a response to the criminal dying alongside him on the cross. The criminal said, "Jesus, remember me when you come into your kingdom." Jesus responded, "Truly I tell you, today you will be with me in paradise" (Luke 23:42-43). Jesus promised his eternal presence on the other side of death, so we ought to as well. I suppose I fear simple answers as a quick fix to the real agony and anguish that death brings. In the end, our declaration that Grandpa Melvin is with Jesus does not nullify the heartache and suffering his death brings to his family and friends. In other words, heaven isn't a fix for our pain. It is the place—and by place, I mean the eternal presence and reign of God—where we entrust all things, including our pain.

The kids did not erupt into tears at news of Melvin's death. They were sad, and their countenances had fallen. But I also saw reassurance and hope in their eyes with our Jesus talk. I attribute their hope to the power of the Holy Spirit at work as they learned to hold the tension of death and eternal life together in their minds. Hugs and kisses from their parents also helped; these, too, are avenues of the Holy Spirit's comforting power for parents and kids alike.

Over the next few days, as we prepared for the funeral, we had several similar kinds of talks with the kids. We tried to prepare them for the funeral as well as we could, all the while pointing to the power and promise of Jesus, who now held Grandpa Melvin in his tender mercy and eternal love. We encouraged our kids to ask questions and share their feelings with us. And we tried to sit in the mystery of it all while pointing to the God who raised Jesus from the dead.

A year or so following Melvin's death, our beloved cat Strider died. More accurately stated, I brought Strider to the animal hospital to be euthanized because he was suffering with severe and persistent kidney issues. Strider's death wreaked havoc on our home; all three kids openly wept. They were angry, confused, and devastated. We asked them to say goodbye to our cat of nearly thirteen years before I loaded him in the car. Mostly, the kids just wailed and wiped snot and tears onto Strider's black fur. I did much of the same. With their wailing echoing in my ears, I made the lonely drive with Strider to the destination of his death.

When I returned from the animal hospital, our family convened on one of the girls' beds. I don't remember that it was an intentional move on our part; it just happened. I'll attribute that, too, to the work of Holy Spirit. On the same bed where we shared the news of Melvin's death, our family mourned the death of our family cat. And in our bed conversation, Anya amid her tears asked, "Is Strider with Grandpa Melvin in heaven?" Astoundingly, Anya in her faith journey made the association between her great-grandfather and her cat. Perhaps it was the family grief we shared together that solidified the connection for her. Or maybe the reality of death itself descended upon our family. Or conceivably, the shared location of these impactful conversations triggered her association. How her six-year-old mind was working in that moment will, I suppose, remain a mystery to me.

But into this mystery and the mystery of death, I offered up an answer: "Yes, Strider and Grandpa Melvin are with Jesus in heaven."

+ + +

Grandpa Melvin asked me to preach at his funeral. He said "speak," but I know he meant preach. In recent days, I have tried to remember if he had heard me preach before. I realized he did hear me preach once, at my sister's wedding in 2004. He also heard me say a two-minute reflection at my ordination service—the worship service where I officially became a pastor. That talk was mainly me publicly weeping and thanking God, family, and friends for the journey and support. I do not recall any other time he was at a worship service when I was preaching. In our family, the farmers in rural Minnesota do not find themselves in the Twin Cities all that often. The demands of the farm leave little room for weekend excursions for anything, let alone attending a worship service in Minneapolis. This is understood by all in the family.

Melvin was trusting I would be able to say something of significance at his funeral, I think, despite his lack of experience with my preaching. The truth is that his request was not about my skill as a preacher but more so my relationship to him and the family. I am his grandson and, as it turns out, a preacher as well. Familiar faces during significant transitions are often desired to bring comfort amid discomfort, stability in the throes of instability. No other pastor on the planet would be as familiar to the ten children, thirty-four grandchildren, and thirty-five great-grandchildren of Melvin and Ellen than I. That's just a fact.

The pastor of the town church my grandparents joined when they moved off the farm was not a familiar face. He was, in fact, an interim pastor. Their regular pastor had recently taken another call to another church in another town; he had moved on. The interim pastor—the person who faithfully pastors a congregation while the members search for a new permanent pastor—was a retired fellow from another Minnesota town some forty-five minutes away from Appleton. He did his best at tending to my grandfather's dying, making pastoral visits throughout his final weeks. I had empathy for the pastor; many times, I too have been the guy with an unfamiliar face thrust into a sensitive pastoral situation. It's never an easy task.

Grandma Ellen took her children Vivian (my mother and her child number one), Rodney (number three), and Renae (number ten and, incidentally, only two years older than my brother) with her to plan the funeral with the interim pastor. Sadly, there was not much wiggle room in the worship planning for my grandfather's funeral. My grandparents' pastor and church were Lutheran, but a different type of Lutheranism than the church I serve. Although we both trace our teachings back to Scripture and the theological teachings of the sixteenth-century Catholic monk named Martin Luther, we are very distinct. Most notable is this major difference: my Lutheran church body ordains women to be pastors, but my grandparents' church body does not. The difference is rooted in our divergent approaches to biblical interpretation.

When my familial cohort informed the interim pastor of my grandfather's request that his Lutheran-pastor grandson preach at his funeral, the interim said no. His church polity and its approach to Scripture dictated that someone outside the church could corrupt the pure proclamation of the gospel. He refused to let me speak at any point during the worship service, not even to deliver a eulogy.

When my family came out of the funeral-planning session with the pastor, my mom phoned me to tell me the news of "no." The answer came as no surprise to me, and intellectually, I understood it. But emotionally, I was mad as hell. My heart was heavy, my body a little shaky. I kept visualizing Melvin's face before me, free for a moment from his pain when he asked me to speak at his funeral. I kept hearing my dumbfounded "yes"—a promise I had to keep. So I asked my mom for the interim pastor's phone number. I could not let this one go; I could not let my grandfather down. I phoned the pastor.

Though my stomach was churning, I believe I handled myself with calm and integrity in my ten-minute conversation with him. After introducing myself as Melvin's grandson and pastor in the Lutheran church, I kindly asked the pastor to walk through the funeral liturgy for my grandfather. As I listened, I was mentally crafting words that would seek a change of heart.

The moment came. The words sounded a lot like this: "Thank you, Pastor. I believe my grandmother, Ellen, and my mom, Vivian, told you about my grandfather's request to have me preach at his funeral. Here is the thing about my grandfather: He was a stubborn German farmer his whole life long. He never asked anything from me. Never—except this one thing. His dying request of me was to preach at his funeral. I know our Lutheran churches are different in polity and practice, but we both adhere to proclamation of Christ crucified and risen. My grandfather asked me to preach, so I'm asking you: can I preach?"

And his response sounded like this: "Your family did share with me the request. And I just can't do that. We did talk about maybe having you say a few words of remembrance before the funeral begins."

With tears welling in my eyes and a wobble in my voice, I reiterated along these lines: "With all due respect, my grandfather asked me to preach. And to do everything I can to fulfill his dying wish, I need to ask you one more time: can I preach at Melvin's funeral?"

"No. I'm sorry. But I will allow you to address those present before the funeral starts."

I remember thanking the pastor for hearing my request and allowing me to speak before the funeral started, even though the butterflies in my stomach had turned to daggers. It hurt hard, and I felt as if I were letting my grandfather down. But while still on the phone, I had a flash of realization. Who cares?! Who cares *when* I speak? The fact is I get to speak! And isn't that what Melvin asked—that I speak at his funeral? Everyone would be gathered, his casket would be there, the church candles would be lit, and I would be standing at a microphone with words to say. Semantics be damned, I was going to fulfill my grandfather's dying request.

Following my realization, I told him, "Well, I'm a preacher. So I will use a Bible passage for my words of remembrance." He responded, "That's fine." I thanked him again for listening to me and for the opportunity to speak, and we hung up.

A smile crept across my face. A sermon is a sermon, no matter if it is before, during, or after the worship service. I was going to fulfill the only request my grandfather had made of me in our shared thirty-eight years of life: I was preaching at Melvin's funeral.

+ + +

I have always cherished the preaching task—at least, generally speaking. I have certainly had agonizing moments of sermon writing followed by sermon delivery excruciating for all involved. That's the gig. Not every sermon is a home run, and sometimes you pray you'll be hit by the pitch so you can limp to first base. Yet the task and charge to preach are what pulled me into this vocational ministry.

With that said, I haven't always been a fan of children's sermons. I often questioned their efficacy and wondered if they were more of a distraction *from* worship than a component *of* worship. I have said more than once, "We don't call all the worshippers over sixty-five years old to come forward, make them sit on the floor, ask them questions that test their Bible acumen, and then laugh at them when they summon the courage to speak." I'm not sure this was the best argument for dropping children's messages from the liturgy, but I have seen many kids physically deflate when their earnest responses conjure the cackles of the congregation. Worship leaders, Sunday-school teachers, youth minsters, and pastors must be careful not to unintentionally and ever so publicly shame our children. For many reasons, then, I have tried worming my way out of delivering children's sermons, especially early in my ministry.

But when I had children of my own, I learned to see worship through their eyes. I learned to look at the liturgy through the faith of my kids. What I have seen is that my kids thoroughly enjoy the children's messages at our congregation, and not just because their dad is *not* delivering them (although that may be part of it, too). Because I am now a pastor in a college and graduate-school setting, children's messages are no longer my responsibility. At my congregation, the pastors, deacon, high-school students, and other adults who give the children's messages do an outstanding job. They create a welcome environment, are sensitive to the needs of the children, teach on a plethora of topics, and instill in the kids a sense of belonging in worship. My children enthusiastically scamper to the center of our worship space when beckoned to receive a word of God for them in the midst of our intergenerational worship. I get goosebumps watching my young son wiggle his way to sit next to his big sisters.

So, thanks to my children and my home congregation, my appreciation for children's sermons has grown. Our church has one every single week, no matter what. It is one of the many ways they communicate full welcome and participation of children throughout the entire service. And it speaks volumes to children about their own place in the midst of worshipping assembly. I fully realized the importance of children's messages when Melvin died and we were preparing for his funeral.

As a pastor and a parent, I have heard many people question the presence of children at funerals. Two arguments advocating for the absence of children from funerals tend to surface. The first, out of concern for the well-being of the kids, says a funeral is too much for them to handle. The curiosity and questions of little ones alone are enough to make adults quarantine kids from funerals. The other reason to exclude kids is, well, that they're kids. They are loud and squirmy and fussy from time to time, so they present a potential disruption of a sensitive time of grief. Each parent has to decide what is best for their family and how much their child(ren) will participate in funeral liturgies and rituals surrounding death. But I believe with all my parenting heart that children need to be at funerals. Children need to confront the truth of death, learn to grieve in community, be recognized and supported in their own pain, and ultimately hear the eternal promise of God's love in Christ Jesus for them and for those who have died.

Without question, our three children (ages six, four, and one at the time) were going to be in worship at my grandfather's and their great-grandfather's funeral in rural Minnesota. As a family and as people of faith, we needed to grieve and worship God together. Two days before the funeral, I was explaining the funeral worship service to my two older daughters. After hearing about the casket, that there would be singing and Bible readings, and that our whole family would be together at my grandfather's church, my eldest daughter, Anya, immediately asked, "Is there going to be a children's sermon?" I was floored. I'd never before thought about having a children's sermon at a funeral—not once. And I think about funeral liturgies a lot! Her question serves as a testimony to me of the import of children's messages in the lives of the young believers in our communities of faith. I fumbled my way, trying to fashion a response that made sense as to why they weren't going to hear a children's message. All I could really say was "No, there isn't a children's sermon at Great-Grandpa Melvin's funeral." These words felt entirely inadequate.

Of course, there wasn't a children's sermon at my grandfather's funeral. Maybe there should have been. I would have been happy to preach that one! Granted, given the circumstances regarding my effort to preach at Melvin's funeral, I know such an effort would have been unsuccessful. But if I had followed Anya's wisdom and had I been in an environment that supported my participation in the funeral liturgy, here's what I imagine I would have done for the children's sermon. It would have been simple and saturated with gospel promise. I would have gathered all thirty-five great-grandchildren around my grandfather, asked them to place their hands on the casket, and had them repeat after me:

"Great-Grandpa Melvin," [repeat]

"Jesus loves you" [repeat]

"Today, tomorrow, and forever." [repeat]

Then I would have looked at them and said, "Dear ones, the Jesus who loves Great-Grandpa Melvin loves you, too—today, tomorrow, and forever. Amen."

+ + +

Graveside, I tightly held Svea's hand. Her four-year-old eyes were fixed on Grandpa's casket as the funeral-home director and groundskeeper had been unexpectedly called upon to lower Melvin into the rich black Minnesota soil. I admit that I wanted desperately to know what Svea's little mind was thinking, but the sacred silence kept my meddling words at bay. Under that bright, bluebird summer sky, father and daughter's sweat-clasped hands held firm as we accompanied my grandfather all the way to the grave. The significance of that day's moment, forever kept in my heart, was precipitated by whole familial experience of faith in the face of death.

For following the funeral service and basement luncheon at the bigger town church, cars snaked through the countryside in procession on the way to the small country church less than two miles from the family farm. The cars kicked up dust from the dirt road that ran through farmland skirting the edge of the church property. Like a sentinel on the plain, this small white church kept watch with its steeple and squat bell tower reaching up toward the heavens on a cloudless summer day. The gorgeous sight of farm and faith melded together were emblematic of the sustenance that had fed this rural community throughout the decades. Through corn and soybeans, the caravan followed the hearse that drove Melvin through his country one last time.

This small, picturesque church was where my grandfather had been nurtured in his faith for all but the last few years of his life. It had been the family church for well over a century. As was the practice in earlier days, the church used to have a one-room schoolhouse on the property as well. It was there that Melvin completed his schooling through eighth grade, taking to the farm full-time thereafter. This was the home of many family baptisms, confirmations in the faith, weddings, and burials. In fact, my parents were married in this little church nearly forty-five years ago. For all of us, it was a sacred site, harboring memories of ritual moments marking time and transitions. The dust cloud from the dirt road signaled to the lonesome church in the field that she was needed again.

As the hearse shepherded our parade of vehicles to the church, we parked on the grass field directly south of the building. Our arrival was met with the ringing of the bell. Wafting out over the prairie, the one-tone bell welcomed Melvin and his accompanying community of family and friends to the burial. Like the days of old, the church bell signaled to its people a moment of significance in the life of her beloved. It was a call that reverberated around us and within us. Replaying that sound in my ear as I write this makes me think about Will Thompson's late-nineteenth-century hymn "Softly and Tenderly, Jesus

Is Calling," because, well, churchy stuff has seeped into my soul, and I can't escape it. The hymn's refrain places words on the lips of Jesus proclaiming to us:

> "Come home, come home!
> You who are weary, come home."
> Earnestly, tenderly, Jesus is calling,
> calling, "O sinner, come home!"

The bell of the church carried us grief-weary sinners to the home of the living promise of Christ Jesus that now called Melvin out from death into eternity. Thus, we accompanied Melvin to the completion of his earthly journey all the way to his end at the church's cemetery.

In light of today's death-defying culture, a cemetery less than twenty yards from a church building might be seen as morbid and off-putting. After all, these days, who wants to go worship and stare death in the face? Worship, generally speaking, has been packaged to us as an entertainment hour, a full-on feel-good celebration that serves almost as escapism from the hardships of daily living. There's nothing like the persistent reminder of death to kill the buzz of a party! But despite cultural trends, the church is called to live the truth of life *and death* as people united to the life, death, and resurrection of Jesus. And this country church's cemetery set in stone—tomb stone—reveals both theologically and architecturally death's constant claim upon the lives of those who have come to worship over the decades. And here's how:

The cemetery is located immediately behind the church. Since I had been in the church sanctuary numerous times, I knew that the Communion table was pushed up against the far wall. Around the table is a semicircular wooden communion railing, where during worship services, people kneel to receive the sacrament of Holy Communion, the real presence of Christ Jesus in the word, wine, and wheat. When people come to the table to partake of the bread and wine, they see people gathered around half of the table set against the wall. But in truth, the living saints of God are invited to feast with the saints who have died in Christ. You can see this in your mind's eye if you imagine the far wall of the church removed. The full circle around the table is completed by the graves of deceased believers. Seen in its fullness, it is a table for the living and dead.

This is the real party—a true celebration in communion with the saints throughout time, living and dead. To be sure, we are all marked by death. Like a leaky diaper oozing down our arm, death sticks to our bodies—except, unlike poop, death cannot be washed off. We are all stained with the stink of death, but herein lies the power of Christ's welcome table. Together, in death and in life, the communion of saints is called to feast on the grace of Jesus, tasting the hope of life everlasting. It is a summons, a homecoming welcome to the divine dinner table. And I believe the dinner table of heaven is a fully intergenerational table, where the saints of all ages belly up to the meal of grace for all eternity. For here, as at every table hosted by Jesus, comes the soft and tender call to all children, parents, grandchildren, and citizens of heaven—all of us: "Come home, weary ones, come and receive life in me." Too often, the church gets it wrong and needs to reform its architectural space, but at other times, the church's theology codified in stone is right and salutary, directing us to the divine goodness of God. That was the case with the cemetery and table of all the saints at this little farm church in rural Minnesota.

The bell rang out. Grandchildren from six of the ten family units carried Melvin to the hole in the ground, waiting to receive him. Somberly and with unified strength, they placed his coffin on the metal lowering device directly over the freshly dug grave. Melvin was now suspended over his resting spot by strong polypropylene straps—the same kind of straps used to tie something down onto the top of a car or trailer. I remember the deafening silence of that moment. I'm not sure if all thirty-five great-grandkids were at the grave in the summer sun. I didn't count, but kids were everywhere. And they, too, were miraculously quiet, as the littler ones in particular clung to family members with questioning eyes.

Soren, our one-year-old at the time, had fallen asleep in the car on the ride to the country church. His catnap contributed to the graveside quiet, no doubt. Melanie stood near enough to the door-ajar vehicle to monitor Soren while still being part of the grave gathering. Svea was with me, and Anya found her Grandpa Jim's hand. Anya's gesture was a testament to the way my parents have been amazing grandparents to my children. While my mother was near her mom, sharing their grief together as mother and daughter, my father was sharing his grief with his granddaughter. It was altogether a holy moment of parenting in faith for us all! Collectively, the great-grandkids sensed the gravity of what our family was doing together and responded. I think the silence was part confusion and part awe as we all wrestled with the mystery of death. The stillness was necessarily interrupted by the pastor, who led us in a brief though ancient practice of Christian burial: Scripture readings, prayers, the Lord's Prayer, and a final blessing over the dead sinner-saint.

The quiet was then significantly magnified when the pastor's final amen was prayed. It was as if death were taking a long, cold stare back at our family. In the open prairie, we were caught in death's gaze with nowhere to hide. The seconds elongated to minutes. No one wanted to leave or break the heavy hush cast upon us all. Fittingly, my grandmother was the first to speak. Though she spoke in a near whisper, we all heard her—not her muffled words, but the sound of her voice. The pastor leaned close to listen to Ellen. Within moments, he called the funeral director, Jason, into the conversation. What my grandmother said surprised Jason and the pastor.

A small-town aside: Jason's sister was my Aunt Jodi. Jodi married Mike, the number-eight child of Melvin and Ellen. In the spring of 1994, Jodi had tragically died a few days after the birth of their second daughter. Jodi's grave was not far from where we stood. That was an altogether different heartache that has marked our family and the community. So Jason is like family. That's rural Minnesota; folks are deeply connected.

Though I couldn't hear my grandmother's words, the body language of Jason and the pastor communicated that her words had caught them off guard. Whatever she had said clearly was not part of the funeral preplanning sessions. With the side conversation over, the pastor stated to us all, "Ellen has requested to stay while the casket is lowered into the ground. She also said that people are welcome to leave if they wish." For me, that was the moment of all the day's treasured moments that shone the brightest with beauty and grace.

My grandmother, a farmer's wife at fifteen and a farmer in her own right, had declared that she wasn't going to leave her beloved until he was put into the earth, the same earth they had together cultivated the whole of their lives. The Minnesota soil that took Melvin's sweat and blood for some eight decades would now take his whole body back to itself. And Ellen wanted to see it through, to return her husband back to the ground from which we all come. For the God of our beginning, as confessed in the book of Genesis, breathed the Spirit into dust and dirt to create humankind. We are dust, and to dust we shall return. Or as stated often in Christian burial at a grave, "Ashes to ashes, dust to dust." Melvin then, like all of us one day, was destined to return to dust.

It may seem odd that a pastor and funeral director would be

surprised at a request to actually bury someone at a Christian burial service. But what I have experienced in today's death-defying culture is a reluctance to complete the task. It is, after all, physically awkward and emotionally challenging to lower a casket into the ground. The common practice I have typically witnessed is that people leave the casket sitting aboveground after what needed to be said has been said. When the people have dispersed, then the groundskeepers and funeral directors (and sometimes the pastors) complete the burial. When my grandmother reclaimed this part of the burial process for our family, my heart sang with gratitude.

Jason called the groundskeeper to assist him in lowering the casket, using the polypropylene straps. They did it. Sweating in the midafternoon heat, two men inelegantly though reverentially completed the unexpected performative act. It was raw and real; it was death. But by their hard work, our family through the bequest of my grandmother completed the journey with Grandpa Melvin. I made a point to thank the groundskeeper and Jason for the sublime gift they had given my family and me that day. And some months later, I phoned Grandma Ellen to tell her how faith-edifying her request to bury Grandpa had been for me. I simply could not sit on my gratitude for that sacred moment that I will take with me to my own grave.

I don't know what parenting in faith always looks like, and I am certain I flub it up more times than not. But at the grave with Svea's four-year-old fingers woven with mine, I was near certain that parenting in faith looks exactly like burying Melvin together. Grandma Ellen was, after all these years, still parenting in faith her ten children. My folks were parenting and grandparenting in faith with their tears and prayers. And I believe Melanie and I were parenting in faith together as we held our children close in the shadow of death. Grief and wonder, sadness and memory, uncertainty and hope, death and life—all of it and all of us were held in the never-failing grip of God's eternal promise. As I recall Svea's hand in mine, I hope her memory will hold a piece of this powerful experience of faith in the face of death. The sound of the church bell, perhaps? The smell of freshly dug soil? The sight of family members crying? The feeling of my perspiring hand desperately, lovingly clutching hers? I'm not sure what, if anything, she will remember. But as a parent, I have faith.

When the burial was complete, eventually the stillness ceased. Children must be children, after all. So, what next? Games and merriment, of course! Anya and Svea found their same-age cousins, Mason and Myles (my sister's boys), and some sort of chasing game began. They cajoled their older tween and teenage cousins, Griffin, Ashton, and Hudson (my brother's boys), to join them. Those kids ran throughout the gravestones with smiles and laughter, a testimony to the communion of saints as the dead experienced the dance of the living on their graves. I remembered again the Communion table inside the church on the other side of the church wall, completing this circle. Life and death together, as it should be, with Christ Jesus leading us all to the edge of eternity in that very moment.

I wanted to join the kids' game and skip through graveyard with them, allowing bodily grief to give way to joy. Instead, I watched sixteen-year-old Griffin scoop up his four-year-old cousin Svea and spin her around, her church dress gleaming in the summer sun. Simply stunning! And I prayed, "I hope to God she remembers this moment."

Final Word

logos (noun): Ancient Greek, meaning "word"; 1. in Greek philosophical thought, the defining principle that shaped the universe; 2. the divine word of God, as written in the Gospel of John: "In the beginning was the *logos*, and the *logos* was with God, and the *logos* was God" (1:1); 3. the Word of God incarnate—Jesus Christ.

There is no final word in parenting, because the work is never finished. Even after the children are tucked into bed and the last good night is uttered, there are still tasks to do, thoughts to be considered, and likely more words to be spoken ("Hey! Get back to bed. You have school tomorrow"). Parenting is a twenty-four-hour-a-day gig, they say. They are right. And the same is true of faith. Faith in God and God's promises is an ongoing journey of doubt and confidence, of pain and joy, of despair and hope, of lamentation and praises unto our God. When it comes to parenting and faith, there are no endings in sight, only brief moments of respite along the way. So to offer up a "final" word on parenting in faith seems presumptuous, if not foolhardy. Yet here I am.

Please consider these brief final reflections not as definitive thoughts on the topic but as some ideas I have gleaned from my own journey. I welcome you to receive them as strength for your journey in faith, or in parenting, or in parenting in faith. Because you have heard my story, you know one thing for certain: I am no expert. I am simply a preacher-parent who believes with my whole heart that God calls us all to preach the love of God while serving others—especially while loving and serving the children in our lives. And as we do so, God's grace is revealed in and through the youth and young ones among us. Ultimately, children become the best teachers of the faith by sharing the love of Jesus with us, if we but listen and watch and wonder alongside them. These are the stories to cherish and share with one another, for these are stories that enliven our faith as people of God and empower us to share God's grace with all of God's beloved children.

With that, here are a few final words on parenting in Christian faith:

- **Parenting in faith is messy.** I don't have to convince parents that parenthood is a mess of poop and vomit and snot and unidentifiable stuff. Bodies are messy things. From the first breath in the delivery room, a child enters the world amid messiness. This we know. But what is sometimes lost on us is the truth that our God is an embodied God. Amid the shit of it all, God is present. Our bodily brokenness is affirmed by our God, who meets us in Jesus—the *Logos* of God in the flesh. And a God who shows up in our messes is a God who is all in with us.

- **Parenting in faith is holy.** Children and faith are both gifts given by God. Yes, the delivery room is messy, but it is also sacred ground, as God-given life is birthed into the world. And we as parents, grandparents, aunts or uncles, godparents, neighbors, friends, and community members are all invited into the sacred task of caring for the children among us. When we honor the children among us, we honor God. As Jesus proclaimed, "Whoever welcomes one such in my name welcomes me" (Mark 9:35). This is holy ground; this is parenthood.

- **Parenting in faith is communal.** I know that I cannot parent alone, nor can I believe in God on my own. I need family, friends, and a community of believers to sustain me. I have learned this more so as parent leaning into the wisdom, support, and experiences of others. And I know that without my worshipping communities throughout the years, my faith would have dried up. I pray that parents have compassion for themselves and seek compassion from others as we share this nonstop journey of parenting in faith together.

- **Parenting in faith is a call.** Vocation is the fancy church word used, but I really do believe God gives us unique gifts and abilities for the well-being of the world. In the waters of baptism and by God's own *Logos*, we are claimed anew as God's own. Our identity therefore is in God, who calls us to serve and love in Christ's name. And parenting the children among us is a primary way we use our God-given gifts for loving service and care. We are called by God to parent.

When I was still an every-Sunday preacher serving in Minneapolis, our girls were little tykes. They loved to run around the huge sanctuary space after worship. I'm sure they would have rather run around the space *during* worship, but Melanie, as an expert pew parent, kept them (mostly) contained. Post-worship running was obligatory in order to let out pent-up energy and allow the girls to enjoy the long aisles that made for great chasing lanes.

Following the service on one particular Sunday, the girls were stomping around the space, as was their practice. It was the summer Svea was turning two. As a late walker, Svea wasn't the most skilled of runners but did her best to keep up with her older sister. As they ran around with wild abandon, I was heading to my office to put away my robe and tidy up from the morning. I caught a glimpse of Svea darting up to the pulpit in her darling blue church dress, with her hair all curled up from the humidity of Minnesota's summer. She had a bink in her mouth, because the Bink Fairy still had a few months or so before her arrival. I followed her to the pulpit to see what mischief she was concocting.

As I came around the back of the large pulpit, Svea was tentatively climbing the three steps to get in it. Like a mountaineer reaching the summit, Svea turned around and looked at me with a sense of pride and accomplishment. After a brief pause, she popped her pacifier out of her mouth with her right hand, flung her arms wide as if to share a hug, and shouted, "Jesus!"

Jesus.

If ever there is a final word in parenting in faith, this is it. *Jesus*, spoken on the lips of my child. Svea knew at nearly two years of age that the pulpit was a place people (her dad!) talk about Jesus, the *Logos*, the Word of God made flesh. And she, in her faith, was now preaching that word to me! Truth be told, it was the best sermon ever preached from that pulpit.

My heart burst that summer morning, and to this day, I'm still finding pieces of love and joy all over the place. The *Logos* had entered into the beautiful mess of parenting in the Christian faith—and did so with one word on the lips of a child: *Jesus*.

Acknowledgments

This project of mine has been buoyed by many dear saints, whether they know it or not. My parents, Vivian and James, parented me in faith; I learned the words and songs of the faith as a child alongside my brother and sister because my parents brought us to church. Along with God, my parents are responsible for me becoming a pastor. The congregations of Pilgrim Lutheran Church (Saint Paul, Minnesota), Good Shepherd Lutheran Church (Woodstock, Georgia), and Bethany Lutheran Church (Minneapolis, Minnesota) each called me to serve as their pastor for a time and trusted me to preach Jesus while serving alongside them; I am deeply grateful. In particular, I give thanks to God for Rev. Dr. Paul Wisdom Baumgartner and Deacon Michelle Angalet at Good Shepherd Lutheran Church, who supported Melanie and me in our heartache and our joy as we sought to become parents. I continue to be thankful for my collaborative colleague and trusted friend at Augsburg University, Rev. Sonja Hagander. She never read a word of this thing, but she knew I was working on "something." That was enough for her to mention my name to my now editor, Lisa Kloskin. Without Sonja and subsequently Lisa, this project would still be hanging out on my computer's hard drive. Gratitude abounds for my preaching mentor, Rev. Dr. Anna Carter Florence, whose first question to me was always "How are your babies?" Dr. Florence's constant question demonstrated for me what our priorities as preacher-parents should be.

Also, I am ever thankful to Edina Community Lutheran Church and its faithful leaders, including Rev. Stephanie Coltvet Erdmann, Rev. Erik Strand, and Deacon Lauren Morse-Wendt. The congregation welcomed and affirmed our children as full participants in the life of our faith community. In honoring the faith of the children in our church community, they honor God.

Early on, I had two unofficial editors who read some rough pages and believed they were worth sharing: Amy Hanson, for eight years my editor in all things church, who was the first to read much of this content, and Ellie Roscher, who said, "This is a book; keep writing!" Thank you both. Also, my thanks to Rev. Justin Boeding, who took a look at some early pages and offered words of encouragement. To my parent-pastor peer group, Rev. Jen Nagel, Rev. Brad Froslee, Rev. Laurie Eaton, and Rev. Jay Carlson: you all have walked with me for years, sharing laughter, wisdom, tears, and many prayers as we all live out our calls to preach and parent. It has been my privilege and joy to share these callings with you, my dear friends.

And finally, thanks to my children, Anya Grace, Svea Vivian, and Soren James. You love me despite my failings as your dad and have gifted me with grace upon grace. And to my partner in parenting and companion in this pilgrimage of faith, my beloved, Melanie, what can I say? We have these three God-given treasures together, and my heart is so very full because of you.

Amen. Thanks be to God!

On the Nativity of Our Lord 2017